T0156482

My Four Score and Ten Years

My Four Score and Ten Years

✦

Memories through the Eyes of a Husband,
Father, Grandfather, Professor,
and World Traveler…

James Westbrook Drury

iUniverse, Inc.
New York   Bloomington

My Four Score and Ten Years
Memories through the Eyes of a Husband, Father, Grandfather,
Professor, and World Traveler...

Copyright © 2010 by James Westbrook Drury

All rights reserved. No part of this book may be used or reproduced by
any means, graphic, electronic, or mechanical, including photocopying,
recording, taping or by any information storage retrieval system without the
written permission of the publisher except in the case of brief quotations
embodied in critical articles and reviews.

The views expressed in this work are solely those of the author and do not
necessarily reflect the views of the publisher, and the publisher hereby disclaims
any responsibility for them.

iUniverse books may be ordered through booksellers or by contacting:

iUniverse
1663 Liberty Drive
Bloomington, IN 47403
www.iuniverse.com
1-800-Authors (1-800-288-4677)

Because of the dynamic nature of the Internet, any Web addresses or links
contained in this book may have changed since publication and may no longer
be valid.

ISBN: 978-1-4502-1074-4 (sc)
ISBN: 978-1-4502-1072-0 (dj)
ISBN: 978-1-4502-1073-7 (ebk)

Printed in the United States of America

iUniverse rev. date: 3/3/2010

This book is for my family; my wife, our children and grandchildren, and their children yet to come.

"All the world's a stage and all the men and women merely players …"

William Shakespeare
As You Like It: Act 2 Scene 7

Table of Contents

Part 5.   *Friends and Others*

Part 6.   *Lawrence, Door County and Later Years*

Part 7.   *Travels*

Part 8.   Reflections and Retirement

Part 9.   Timeline

Acknowledgements

The text is mine, but I am much indebted to:

Danelle Drury, my granddaughter, for her patience, informed typing and selecting of the pictures.

Meris Barnes, for her thoughtful typing.

Jane Drury, Ann Heyse, Jon Drury and Eleonora Drury, my children, for their assistance in editing.

Jerry Niebaum, my colleague and friend, for his encouragement and his computer expertise in this endeavor.

My dear wife, Danny, for her great assistance in remembering dates and events.

Preface

Words, words and more words — are the basic tools of all authors. This manuscript has evolved from being an autobiography to being my memoirs.

At 90 I look back at a happy, full life with only a few "bumps." My wife and I have been happy and feel that KU has been supportive, allowing leave for us to do "our thing." There have been pot-holes, but I decided to omit them.

Why a memoir? I consider it important for future sociology teachers and students to know how at least one regular guy like me adjusted to his situation. Also, this collection of stories is intended as a memento for my children and grandchildren and extended network of family and friends. I suspect that having been a college professor and having taught at only one university has affected my perceptions. Those who have taught at more than one university would not have developed a strong loyalty to their "home" University. My loyalty to KU has influenced my views.

PART 1

My Ancestors

My grandfather,
Dr. Henry Naltinus Drury (Drewry).

My grandfather, Henry Naltinus Drury was born on November 29, 1847 in Switzerland County, Indiana. He lived on a farm there until the age of fifteen. He studied at the Industrial University of Champagne, Illinois.

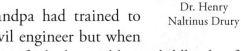

Dr. Henry
Naltinus Drury

He volunteered to go on the train to Chicago to help put out the great Chicago fire in 1871.

Grandpa had trained to be a civil engineer but when his first wife died, possibly in childbirth, after only a year of marriage, he attended the Rush Medical Clinic in Chicago and became a medical doctor.

He then married my grandmother, Mary Mann. They had two children, Jean Paul Drury - my father - and Lillian Lucille Vernon nee Drury, my aunt.

Hettie Drury,
Henry's first wife

County records show that Dr. Drury practiced medicine in Altamont, Illinois. Altamont is a small farm town in the western part of Effingham County in the central part of Illinois.

Mary Mann Drury

In the 1890's there were no electric lights, no TVs, no automobiles, and the world moved much more slowly. Henry, my grandfather, was a practicing medical doctor who made his calls in a horse-drawn buggy. It went slowly —about three miles an hour. There was one big advantage though. The horse knew the way home. When he finished treating a sick patient, Henry could just start the horse in the right direction, lay the reins in his lap and start getting some much needed sleep.

In Altamont the winters could be severe. My grandmother (Mary Mann Drury) would hear the horse come to the barn and send out young Jean, my father, aged six or seven, to help his father un-harness the horse from the buggy by knocking the ice off the joints of the harness with a hammer.

Henry and his daughter, Lillian on the horse cart

This is the way country doctors practiced medicine in the 1870's. With the coming of the automobile, doctors could more easily make house calls, but they lacked the sophisticated equipment of today to diagnose illnesses.

About 1980, I was traveling in Illinois along Interstate Route 70 with my family and went into Altamont to see the old house where my grandfather had lived. Though it had been years since I had been there, I thought I recognized the angle of the street and the relationship to the railroad line and found the house. I talked to some of the locals and asked who knew the most about the history of the town. I was referred to an eighty- year- old widow who made her living by "taking in boarders," i.e. she cooked for them and had rooms where they slept.

She knew the old Doctor Henry Drury. Once she had been treated by the old doctor when she had diphtheria. Someone in her family had fetched Dr. Drury and he had come out to diagnose and treat her. She remembered that Dr. Drury and her father had spent at least one night at her side and held basins when she had to vomit. Her mother, somehow, was not able to swab her throat, so Dr. Drury showed her father how to do it, and he was able to treat her once the doctor had left. She thought that Dr. Drury had saved her life. This lady recalled that Dr. Drury had brought his son Jean and his daughter Lillian to see her at a later time.

In 1907, when my father, Jean Paul Drury was 20, his mother, Mary Mann Drury died, probably of cancer. She was the one who had been holding the family together. Grandpa deeply mourned Mary's death. He went to the cemetery and sat beside her grave for hours. Probably for a change of scenery he then took an extended trip to Southeast Missouri, leaving Jean to take care of himself and sending Lillian to live with her mother's sister. Henry Drury wrote a document somewhat like a will. It spoke of a guardian (undesignated) for his beneficiaries, Jean and Lillian Drury.

Mary Drury 1905

He gave to the guardian the authority to administer his estate, which was to be used for the advancement and college education of Jean and Lillian. The document has witnesses and was notarized.

In later years when my father and his sister Lillian could no longer care for Henry, he was confined to what in those days was described as the insane asylum. There, I have been told, he was allowed to doctor other patients.

On April 4, 1921, Henry Drury died at the Asylum in Alton. The hospital asked for instructions for burial. Presumably he was buried in Altamont.

My father, Jean Paul Drury
1887-1964

On October 4, 1887, Jean Paul Drury was born in Altamont, Ill. There is some conflicting evidence as to the date of his birth. His obituary reported him to be 77 years of age at the time of his death.

Jean Paul Drury 1887

Around the time of Jean's birth, Altamont had about five hundred people and was the center of a farm community. It is about 90 miles east of St. Louis, Illinois, in the flat plains of the eastern part of the Middle West. There were maybe fifty houses in the town. It was an established little community on the main east-west line of the Pennsylvania Railroad.

Jean was not always a model young child. He could be mischievous. In those days there were no supermarkets. Grocery stores would buy things in bulk and then sell small amounts to the local people. People would buy molasses to sweeten food, much as we would use brown sugar today. People in Altamont got their molasses in big barrels, weighing several hundred pounds. These barrels were hard to move. One time, a barrel on the station platform broke and molasses spilled out over some of the platform.

Jean and some of his friends had decided to go down to the railroad station and see the train come in. Some one of the boys, maybe

Jean Paul and Lillian Drury

Jean, got the idea of seeing what would happen if they put molasses on the train track. They got several old brooms and swept the spilled molasses onto the track just ahead of where they expected the engine to stop.

The train came in and stopped to let passengers off and let new ones get on. When the conductor signaled the engineer to start the train, the engineer slowly applied power to the engine and the wheels just spun and kept on spinning, as he applied the throttle. He tried it several times, but still he was not able to start the train.

The conductor and station-master went to talk to the engineer. By this time the boys decided the best thing for them was to disappear. The train stayed in Altamont longer than scheduled; it remained there until the molasses was sanded off the train tracks.

I do not know whether the station-master got in touch with the parents of the pranksters and whether the boys were punished for their prank, but I do know my dad enjoyed telling me this story about his youth.

In 1903, Jean made a trip to St. Louis, to see the World's Fair, celebrating the centennial of the Louisiana Purchase. Almost certainly this was the first big trip Jean made from the small town of Altamont.

Jean attended the Academy of the University of Illinois, in Urbana during 1905 and 1906. Universities ran such academies to qualify students to attend classes at the university. This was almost certainly the case for Jean. He had four semesters at the Academy.

His mother died in 1907. In March 1909, the County Clerk issued a "Letter of Conservatorship," at the request of Jean, who considered his father unable to manage his own affairs, being incapacitated by grief at the loss of his wife. Jean, age 22, was officially appointed Conservator for his father, Henry. In the next term of the Council in February 1910, the Council heard the matter and approved the appointment of Conservator.

In 1918, Jean sent a formal letter to Lillian Drury, Probate Judge in Chamberlain, South Dakota. (This Lillian happened to have the same given name as my aunt Lillian Lucille; the judge was a cousin of my father's.) My grandfather was no longer taking care of his affairs and had left it for Jean to do. Probably in relation to his father's affairs that needed managing, Jean sent her a letter with a report he had filed with the Effingham County Clerk appointing him as the conservator of the estate of "H. N. Drury distracted" – denoting that Grandpa Drury could no longer manage his own affairs.

Without formal training, Jean had picked up telegraphy. He got himself employed as a telegraph operator on the Pennsylvania Railroad, which was the major east-west railroad in that part of Illinois. Under the rules of the Union of Telegraphers contract, he was able to develop seniority and eventually move to more desirable assignments closer to St. Louis.

While working his way to East St. Louis, he boarded with a farm family. The head of the household proposed that Jean settle down on the farm and marry the daughter. While for some it would have been an offer difficult to refuse, Jean turned it down as he was not ready to settle down at that point.

In 1915 Jean married Bernice Boone Taylor in East St. Louis, Ill. Bernice was twenty four and my father was thirty. I think that my parents met at activities for young people, run by their church. They moved into one of the three houses which Alex Taylor, her father, had built on 41st Street. Bernice's parents and her younger siblings lived in the big house. Her eldest brother, Arthur and his wife Marie lived in the bungalow next door to my parents, Jean and Bernice. When Arthur and Marie moved to Detroit, Jean's sister, Lillian, (my aunt) who had married Clinton Vernon, moved into the house they had vacated. By this time my father had started working as an accountant for St. Louis Structural Steel.

Bernice Boone
Taylor Drury

In 1922, an income tax form shows Jean paid $2.89. This tax included farm income tax for the orchard Jean operated as a business with a letter head of "Drury and Makins, Growers and Distributors of Fancy Apples." The income tax report for 1923 is missing, but in 1924, he paid $16.62 tax. My father had inherited the apple orchard from my grandfather, Henry. The apple orchard was in Vevay, Indiana. My father had a manager on site, and I have records from my father pertaining to the storage of barrels that he would sell later in the season at a higher price.

On August 20, 1924, Jean bought the Pearing house in the 1400 block of 40th street, in East St. Louis. This house was a thousand feet closer to the Hawthorne School where I first went to school.

As the bookkeeper-treasurer for the St. Louis Structural Steel, my father's salary was such that when we lived in the Pearing house we had Lydia, an African American wash-woman come in once a week to do the laundry. Lydia was treated pretty much as a member of the family. Years later she would occasionally come to visit my mother in the Law Office in the Arcade Building where my father was then working.

In September 1925, my father quit his job at the St. Louis Structural Steel Company and joined Clinton Vernon, his brother-in-law, in buying a Ford Agency in the small town of Vandalia Mo.— about 60 miles northwest of St. Louis, Missouri. The two families, Drury and Vernon, moved to Vandalia, Mo. My father always said he did this to keep his brother-in-law, Clint, from "losing his shirt." At this time the Ford Company would ship cars to dealers. The dealers were required to take them if they wanted to keep their franchise. Incidentally, this was just the time when Ford started making Model A's and stopped making Model T's. I was told of a conservative farmer who liked the Model T's so well that he bought a second new Model T to store in his barn. He could not believe that the new Model A car could be better.

In 1927, while owning the Ford Agency, Jean made a trip to Springfield, Ill, (the state capital) and took an examination which, together with courses he had taken at the Benton School of Law in St. Louis, qualified him to practice law in Illinois. The Drury family and the Vernon family rented houses in Vandalia, suggesting that they never intended to stay. The Drury family lived in the Kunst House, which was just across the square park adjoining the Ford agency. When it came time to leave Vandalia, my mother and I roomed with Mrs. Bevans, the neighbor, for two or three months to allow me to complete my school year, while my father moved to East St. Louis ahead of us. He had decided to get out of the car sales business and wanted to start a new venture.

Upon leaving Vandalia, my family moved to a small suburban acreage we called the Bluff House adjacent to East St. Louis, Ill. We had a small house and a big chicken house. There were at least a hundred white leghorns — reputedly a good laying strain. Jean was expecting to sell eggs on the side, while practicing law. After a few months in the Bluff House, Jean acquired the 1728 North 48th Street house. The city limits ran down the middle of 48th Street, with the house being in the Village of Washington Park.

Unfortunately my mother never liked the house. It was clearly the least attractive house that my family had ever lived in. Previous houses had been brick and 1728 was a frame house.

1728 as it looks today

In about 1928, my father opened law offices in the Arcade Building in downtown East St. Louis. Clinton Vernon got a Real Estate Broker's license and also got set up to sell insurance — a typical combination in those days. My father and Uncle Clint shared offices and my mother ran the office for both of them. In the same year, Jean ran for a seat in the Illinois state assembly. I am uncertain as to whether he got the Republican nomination or merely ran in the Primary, but this district was strongly Democratic and the Democratic candidate, Mel Price, was elected and served several terms in the Illinois lower legislative house and then many terms in U.S. Congress.

I embarrassed my father. He was an ardent Republican precinct committee man. In Roosevelt's fourth term election, I voted by absentee ballot. When my wife and I next visited St. Louis, the first thing my father asked me was how I could have embarrassed him by voting Democratic. We asked how he could know this, as voting is by secret ballot. He said, "Yes, but there was only one absentee ballot in my precinct and it was a democrat vote and I knew it was yours!"

During this time, the U.SA and the rest of the world were enveloped by the Great Depression. Jean was probably the only attorney who lived in the Village of Washington Park. He applied for the office and was appointed the attorney for the Village. This afforded him one of the few (if not only) retainer fees he could count on each month. The family was glad that they had not extended themselves and bought a more expensive house.

My father's law practice never really made much money. My father told me that what he really enjoyed doing was clearing titles on pieces of property. Sometimes he would buy a piece of property, use his legal expertise to clear the title and then sell it for a profit. He decided the stock market was too volatile for him and so he depended for his income primarily on his rental property in East St.

Jean Paul Drury,
my father

Louis, Ill. For some of the time he owned four, four-family apartment houses (16 units in all.) These were all brick units, which he kept in good shape. They were rented mainly by African American families, and my mother continued to take care of these sixteen rental units for several months after my father died.

Under the United States constitutional legal system in which all alleged criminals are entitled to counsel, my father was assigned to defend, at one point, a man I'll call Mr. X, who had no money to pay for my father's attorney's fee. My father must have won the case as Mr. X did not go to jail and my father allowed him to work out the attorney fee by digging a hole for our sewage box. This was before the Works Progress Administration (WPA) came along that paid men to manually dig out and install sewer systems.

I seem to have inherited my social and extroverted nature from my father. My mother told me that though my father had no formal musical training, he had a good ear and could play almost anything on the piano. He later taught himself to play the violin and sang for many years in the Masonic Men's chorus. He was always the life of a party; he could easily bring good spirits to the group of people around him.

My father lived long enough to get to know all three of his

grandchildren – my three children, and we would visit to and fro for Christmases, Thanksgivings and other such celebrations. My mother and father would drive to Lawrence and after my father's death, my mother would come by bus.

Three generations of Drury men folk - Me, my son Jonathan and my father, Jean

Clint and Lillian would avail themselves of the annual free pass ticket that a retired railroad employee was entitled to. They regularly went to California to visit Aunt Vird – a sister of Mary Mann's. They came to share quite a few holidays with us also. They were on one of their annual visits to Aunt Vird in California when Jean died in 1964. We called them back for the funeral.

My mother,
Bernice Boone Taylor (Drury)

My mother, Bernice, devoted her life to her husband and son. She was born in Pike County, Missouri. The Taylor family lived in the two small cities of Elsberry and Paynesville. I think Bernice was born in Elsberry, but both towns were often mentioned in discussions. My family made infrequent trips to this area to visit cousins — a favorite was Cousin Will Taylor, who lived on a farm not far from Elsberry. Jean was especially fond of the farm-cured ham that they smoked on their farm.

My mother, Bernice Taylor Drury

This was primarily farm country. When visiting there I saw some foundations of the "old slave quarters" which were on the farm where my mother grew up.

My mother completed high school, but I feel confident she had no further formal education. This was in an era when the role of women was in the home. My mother never spoke of jobs she had before she was married. If she had any, they almost certainly were minor clerical office jobs. She did secretarial work to assist my father at the Ford Agency in Vandalia, Missouri and later in his law office.

My parents lived in the 48th Street house until my father died in 1964. My mother stayed on there until she decided to move to Kansas two or three years after my father's death. By the time my father died, my wife Danny and I had settled in Lawrence, Kansas. Mother decided to move to Brewster Place, a retirement home in Topeka. This was especially convenient in the six years that I worked in Topeka, since I could go out to visit with her and have lunch at Brewster Place occasionally. She came to Lawrence for some Saturdays and Sundays. In 1979 Bernice died, just a few weeks after our son Jon and his wife, Liesel, had come from South Africa to see her. Our daughter Ann played her violin at Bernice's funeral service.

Bernice and grandson Jon

Aunt Lillian and Uncle Clint

When my Grandfather Drury's household was dissolved after my grandmother died, Lillian (my aunt) who was about 13 then, went to live with Aunt Jo and Uncle John Howell. Aunt Jo was my grandmother's sister. Lillian grew up in the Howell household and knew the Howell children, Bert and Wayne, much better than my father did.

Uncle Clint and
Aunt Lillian

After leaving Aunt Jo's, Lillian moved to East St. Louis where she met and married Clinton Henry Vernon. The Vernons moved into the bungalow next door to where my parents were living.

Aunt Lillian and Uncle Clint treated me as their child. They had other nephews, but they were in Kentucky. Aunt and Uncle were big people but not obese. Uncle Clint was a car inspector for the railroad for many years. He worked outside on night shifts in all kinds of weather. He would go out in the freezing cold or sweltering heat to decide when a railroad freight car should be repaired or replaced.

Some years later, after Uncle Clint had retired, he would go daily to his stockbroker's office to watch, sometimes intently, the tape showing stock purchases and sales. He liked copper stocks and invested heavily there. Aunt Lillian found out about this and she thought they should sell the stocks and buy Affiliated Mutual in the Lord Abbett Group. This turned out to be a very profitable investment. They willed one half of these stocks to Clint's sister and brother and they gave one sixth of them to my mother, another sixth to Danny, and a sixth to me. Upon my mother's death, her sixth came to Danny and me.

Throughout their lives both Clint and Lillian were frugal and would save for a later day. While working on the railroad, Clint was careful with his finances. He loaned money to his co-workers at an interest. (I'm not sure how legal these loans of his may have been.) This proved to be a profitable venture for him. In retrospect, they were probably too frugal. I remember one day when Aunt Lillian said she needed a new purse and found one she really liked in the store, but would not buy it because she said it was too expensive, even though she could easily have afforded it.

Lillian loved children but never had any of her own. At a time, she was employed by a community service organization in downtown East St. Louis that offered childcare services. She taught first and second grade for a good many years. She liked to take me to the zoo at Forest Park, where we enjoyed the monkey show.

Aunt Lillian believed that when having company for dinner you needed to have two kinds of meat, two kinds of potatoes, two kinds of vegetables, as well as at least two kinds of dessert. One time Aunt Lillian and Uncle Clint invited me to go with them to visit Clint's relatives in Kentucky – Clint had an older and a younger brother. They both lived on farms and it was a treat for me to visit them. They did not have inside plumbing in their homes and while they had passable privies, they would not meet sanitary standards of today.

When Lillian and Clint got to an age where they could no longer manage their finances, I was asked to do it for them. We set up a bank account and I would dole out weekly checks for them to buy their food, despite the fact that they and I were living three hundred miles apart. After Lillian's death, Mrs. Altemeyer, a vigorous older lady care-giver, lived in the house as a housekeeper and took care of Uncle Clint until he died.

PART 2:

Growing Up

James Westbrook Drury

I first saw the light of day about 11:00 AM in my mother's family house on February 22, 1919. Dr. Staunton was there to help. On the day of my birth, my Aunt Lillian had gone to downtown St. Louis to shop in the morning and came home in the afternoon to be surprised to find that I had arrived. I was sufficiently small that they put me in a dresser drawer in lieu of a crib. It was George Washington's formal birthday. I must surely have

James Westbrook
Drury as a toddler

been the object of much attention with grandparents, mother, father, and aunts and uncles not only around, but all living next door.

When I was about two years old, I could recognize a can of corn. I would crawl downstairs to the basement, pick out a can of corn and laboriously bring it up the stairs, hoping to have it for supper. To this day corn is one of my favorite vegetables.

My grandmother,
Elizabeth Taylor

I have always been short in height, measuring about five feet seven as an adult. I was always chosen last and then permitted to play in right field when we played "pick up" baseball.

In 1923 the senior Taylors and their children who still lived at home, moved to California. They sold the larger house to a veterinarian, Doctor Crossland.

When my parents moved to the single family Pearing home, I was close to Hawthorne Elementary School, where I first attended school. In that school students were grouped into a Fall and Spring class. In 1927, when we moved to Vandalia, I was put in second grade in school because they did not have half year classes as in East. St. Louis. Later I attended Lansdowne Junior High School and the white High School near downtown East St. Louis. Schools were segregated in those days, but we never thought much about it – it was just the way things were.

I had very competent teachers. I remember my chemistry teacher, Mr. Scholtz, having our class test the heating capacity of the coal sent by various suppliers to the East St. Louis schools. We would grind up the coal into powder and put it into a grape fruit sized metal container that was air tight. The container would then be submerged in water of a known temperature. We would fire the coal by means of a special device in the sealed container and it would explode – the extent to which it heated the water was measured, and our findings became the basis on which coal was ordered for the whole school district.

Mr. Cook was our physics teacher. He was a very conscientious man, who unfortunately had poor vision in one eye. In those days the copy machines were very primitive. I can remember him standing at an electric powered mimeograph machine, carefully putting sheets of blank paper between each copy, to prevent the ink from smudging or running on the copies he was running for us, his students. My understanding is that only a few high schools in the area offered courses in physics.

I had a course in German with Miss Schmale. In those days languages were not taught with the emphasis on being able to speak them, but rather on being able to read them. I also took a course in typing in high school so as to be able to type when I got to university.

James W. Drury
aged 15 or so

I think I was ranked third in our graduating class of 150 students. I was elected to the honorary society.

My father would trade for anything. In one instance, he bought a small Shetland pony for me, but I did not know how to handle the pony and was not strong enough to make the pony do what I needed him to do. In several days we discovered it was an impossible situation. The pony was sold.

We were back in East St Louis during my high school years. On weekdays the family pattern was for the whole family to leave in the morning and drop me off at High School, 3 miles from our home. I walked or hitchhiked home. On Saturdays I mopped the kitchen and cleaned up the house. At noon my parents would come home, having done the basic shopping for the week. In those days the three of us could barely carry all the groceries that seven or eight dollars would buy.

About 1930, I distinctly remember my family made a major journey to California to visit my grandparents, Aunt Caroline, my Aunt Marsina, and Uncle Dutch and their son, my cousin, Jeff. It took us six days to drive there. On our first day away from our home in East St. Louis, we spent the night in Topeka, Kansas. An unusual aspect of the journey was that we passed through Lawrence, Kansas, where about seventeen years later, Danny and I settled down and have spent most of our lives.

In California, the family made some kind of arrangements for Jeff and me to go through Metro-Goldwyn-Mayer Motion Picture Studios. Our parents thought we should have a manicure. In 2009, I can report that it was the only manicure I have ever had.

Though I cannot remember the precise year, I remember that one time, Uncle Arthur and his wife Marie visited us in East St Louis. On that trip we took them up to some of the areas in Missouri where the senior Taylors, Alex and Liz Taylor had lived. They invited me to return to Detroit with them and I spent the better part

James Drury - High School Graduation

of a summer with them in Detroit and had interesting experiences there. This was in the days before air conditioning, and I remember going with Marie's brother to Belle Isle in the Detroit River, to where it was cooler.

In 1936, when I was 17, my father and his good friend, George Yoxall drove me to the University of Illinois at Champaign-Urbana where I was to study. I lived at various locations, studied much and was able to graduate in three years and a summer session, with a Bachelor of Arts Degree in Political Science. This is in contrast to today, when some students are taking almost five years to get a B.A.

While at the University of Illinois, I took Reserve Officers Training in the Signal Corps. Illinois was one of two universities offering training in codes and ciphers. Now however, coding and ciphering has been transferred to the National Security Agency and it has very broad and expanded controls to safeguard the nation.

Graduate School Replies

The Political Science Department at the University of Illinois, where I had studied, had encouraged me to do graduate work, so they awarded me a scholarship. Thus, for the academic year 1939-40 - my fourth year at Illinois - I had received a $300 scholarship and free tuition. I completed my Master's Degree in June, 1940.

My faculty advisors were all telling me that I should break the ties to my undergraduate institution if I could. I don't feel they wanted to just be rid of me, but they thought I should be exposed to other professors and other ideas. I needed letters of recommendation for all the scholarship and program applications I submitted, and since this was before computers, I could ask my professors to write only so many letters. Somehow, I decided that seven was reasonable. I requested that my professors send letters to four of our biggest and most prestigious universities - Yale, Harvard, Columbia, and Princeton - where I knew the competition would be the stiffest. My remaining applications and professors' letters, I sent where I thought my chances were better—the University of Cincinnati and the University of Minnesota. As a fall-back position, I put in the University of Illinois.

At this time the graduate schools in the U.S. had established the practice of having uniform closing dates and uniform announcement dates. April 1 was that date in 1940.

I stopped at my mailbox after classes and lunch on April 1, 1940, on my way back to my room. Most remarkably, the U.S. Postal Service had cooperated, at least in my case, to deliver all seven answers to my applications, from seven different institutions in different parts of the country, in that one day's mail - one from each of the institutions to which I had applied. I was most excited. I got polite rejection letters from Harvard, Yale, Columbia and Minnesota. I had an award of fellowship at Princeton and a scholarship at the University of Illinois. I was an alternate at the University of Cincinnati.

The choice was not really too difficult - I chose Princeton and wound up getting my Ph.D. degree from Princeton where my senior professor was an acquaintance of the man who later hired me at the University of Kansas. These are the kinds of relationships that determine one's career and future.

My Senior Professor at Princeton, Professor William Carpenter, was a member of the New Jersey Civil Service Commission. He arranged for me to have an internship in the summer for three months at the Civil Service Office. I helped to prepare examinations for people applying for civil service posts. While on this internship, some of the office staff suggested that we go to a special restaurant where in the patrons' part of the restaurant there was a huge oven, and they baked "tomato pies." Now such pies are popular and are known as pizza.

I had finished just one year of my scholarship at Princeton when I was called up for active duty, and my academic life was put on hold for the next five war years. Because of my training in Codes and Ciphers in the Reserve Officer Training Corps at the University of Illinois, I was called to Washington D.C. I had had some limited exposure to the city once before on a debate trip with the University of Illinois.

My father had sensed that the war was coming and had suggested that I go into the ROTC, so that I would not be drafted when war came.

Me sitting on the Dean's lap,
in the academic garb which was required for dinner each evening

Active Army Duty - Apartment 202

The mood in Washington was sober when I first arrived and this intensified after Pearl Harbor when we moved to a six day work week. Despite this, I regard living in Apartment 202 at 2210 Pennsylvania Avenue in Washington, D.C. and meeting the "202 ers" as some of my life's best and happiest experiences.

I had studied in the Signal Corps of the United States Army Reserve Corps (USAR) as a Second Lieutenant and was mustered out as a Major. My friend, Mike March lived in Washington D.C. I knew him from our student days at the University of Illinois. Upon my arrival in Washington, I looked Mike up. He lived with a varying number of young men in a very prestigious location - six blocks from the White House. We referred to that place as Apartment 202. (The whole 202 building has since been demolished.) I temporarily moved into 202.

Lieutenant James Drury

It was quite an adjustment for me to move into the not-too-clean 202 apartment as I was an only child, unused to clutter, and I had just spent a year in the tidy and formal residence hall for graduate students at Princeton. My lodgings were part of my scholarship from Princeton. There I had shared a big suite, approximately 25 by 25 feet, with appropriate study furniture with another young man. There was a fire-place on the inside wall. We shared a bathroom with two other similarly housed male graduate students. Every evening, we wore Master's gowns for dinner - which was preceded by grace in Latin. In Washington D.C., I was looking for a similar place to rent for $100 a month. (In those days the base pay of a second lieutenant was $1800 a year, not a month.)

I don't remember how long I looked to find a similar place somewhere within walking distance of the Munitions Building on Constitution Avenue, about three quarters of a mile walk from Washington Circle. I remember that Lowell Hattery, one of the men at 202, let me know that I should move out or "buy in" by paying $75 for my share of the furniture. So I "bought in."

I tend to remember people in the apartment by where we slept. I think during all of my stay at 202, I had one of the beds in the larger corner bedroom. At a time Mike and H.G. Morrison occupied the other beds. Lowell Hattery and Ted Taylor were in the first bedroom and perhaps Del Ralph moved in with Lowell after Ted moved out.

In the late summer or early fall of 1941, Ted married a girl named Jean Shipley and a car full of us went up to the wedding in upstate New York, including Dale Rogers, Bob Fluno, H.G. Morrison, Del Ralph and myself. We formed the male contingent in the car. Marion (who later married Dale Rogers) was the only woman in the car. At a gas stop an unknown man came up to Marion and asked her as privately as he could if she knew what she was doing going with these disreputable looking "five hombres."

My first job as a Second Lieutenant in the Office of the Chief Signal Officer was to recruit several hundred young civilian women to join the war effort. They were primarily school teachers in the Carolinas and would earn $1600 a year - not a month. We hired an older, dignified and soft-spoken, grandmotherly type to counsel these young women. Her name was Mrs. Golda Watson. One of our employees tried to commit suicide, but many were just homesick, this being their first time away from home for an extended time.

I can remember being in the corner bedroom on December 7, 1941, when the Sunday Symphony was interrupted at about 2:30

to announce the bombing of Pearl Harbor. It was announced later that all military personnel were to report on Monday in uniform. I arrived at my desk in the Munitions Building at 8:00 AM. It took some time for the top commands to get down to my level, but with the nation at war, my office chief felt we had to be covered. Since I was the lowest ranking officer, I drew the night shift. I was relieved Tuesday morning after having done very little all night.

The summers of 1942 and 1943 were noted for several trips to Rehoboth Beach in Maryland. My friends, Shorty and Jessie Ward were sometimes involved. I can remember making many sandwiches for these trips. We'd have six to eight people – two sandwiches a piece – so I would have to make about 16 sandwiches for each trip. How we got gas to go I can't remember. It was closely rationed, as were some foods, including meat and sugar. We all had ration coupon books. On a typical work day, we had very simple breakfasts of milk and cereal, lunch at the office, and we frequently had dinner out. A favorite place was Parklane Cafeteria, a block or so from 202 on Pennsylvania Avenue. Whenever the time came for our ration coupons to expire, we would get our ration books together and get the best meats we could, which were not very choice cuts.

We would have dinners with girl friends invited whenever we had enough coupons. I can remember leaving the Munitions building at 6:00 PM, stopping to buy food, and planning to serve seven or eight people by 7:30 PM. Our small, small dining room was about 8 foot by 8 foot. When we got six to eight people around the table, nothing could really fall on the floor - but we had great times and this was my introduction to quantity simple meal preparation.

On one occasion a number of my friends, young ROTC 2nd Lieutenants from the University of Illinois, arrived in town. None of the 202ers were going to be home so I was free to prepare a meal for the Lieutenants. I prepared a meal for six people. We were so cost conscious that it never occurred to me to pick up the tab. I fed them for a total of $1.00 and I charged each of my guests 16 cents. We had pork butt steaks, boiled potatoes, some vegetables, and chocolate pudding. In the 1940's we bought *six* boxes of Mighty Fine pudding mix for a quarter.

Our accounting book was simple. Everyone could buy supplies and enter the amount they spent in the book - if they remembered. Everyone was entitled to eat whenever a meal was served and at month's end each paid their share for meals whether they had been there or not. At the end of the month each person's share of the rent was added to food costs and a total arrived at. From this amount, whatever we had recorded as having paid for food was subtracted, and then we each paid our share.

Mike March became famous, or should I say infamous, for serving the very nutritious combination for dessert of stewed apples and raisins every time he cooked. Maybe we finally persuaded him to try something else. Kitty Morrison complimented me on my apple pies. She thought the secret was that my hands were bigger and that I could shape the dough better. I thought adding *cold* water helped.

There was one interval when Dave Brown got interested in adding food dyes and coloring to our otherwise wholesome food, in colors that few of us could tolerate. One time Kitty was stirring something on the stove when Dave distracted her and put in some blue dye. When she returned to stirring, she found the corn turning blue.

I have many memories of events at 202. One is seeing, from our vantage point overlooking the sidewalk, a group of policemen maneuvering a drunk into the waiting paddy wagon without any of the policemen really touching him. Another was Ted's practice of sleeping on dirty sheets. This did not bother him, because he took a bath every morning. (We had no shower.) I can picture Frank Shea sitting at the dining table in the morning with his mirror, shaving his beard.

Once we had a vacancy in 202 and advertised with all kinds of prerequisites such as a Master's in Public Administration. When the day came that the ad ran in the paper, there was no one there to answer the phone. Another amusing phone incident occurred when I was promoted to First Lieutenant. The rules were such that the higher pay took effect only after an officer took the oath of office for the higher grade. The personnel office, trying to be helpful, called to tell me that I had been promoted. This happened at a time when the phone was being answered as though it was a dairy. The office was informed that Lieutenant Drury was out on a milk run.

Our friends, the 202-ers, have been constant in our life, and have led to many happy parties.

I made a point of staying active in the Reserves in order to be sure that I would qualify for the USAR retirement pay. Having had more than 5 years of active duty and then sixteen more years of Active Reserve Duty, I qualified. I stayed active and commanded a little Strategic Intelligence Research and Analysis Team (the 468th SIRA Team) and in time was promoted and was a Full Colonel when I retired.

My Wife

Danny has been my most loyal supporter and thoughtful critic.

It is through 202 that I met Florence Mary Daniels, who became my wife. There were three "Florences" in her sorority when she was in college. To distinguish between the three for telephone calls she became known as "Danny." The name has stuck and is used by all who know her.

Danny and me in Washington

We met on a Saturday night in October of 1942, on a blind date arranged by H.G. Morrison's fiancée, Kitty Adkins (Morrison.) We were introduced in her Hertford Place apartment. Danny was wearing a deep navy blue two-piece dress. I made it my business to get her telephone number. Probably on Sunday night, I telephoned and asked her to come with me to the Balalica Restaurant on Connecticut Avenue.

Her Uncle Rex was in Washington as a Navy officer. I think Danny's parents arranged for Uncle Rex to check me out. I vaguely remember that Uncle Rex, his wife, Danny and I went out to dinner at a seafood restaurant. Fortunately, I must have passed, for she kept seeing me.

Thus began a courtship that lasted a year. I proposed to her and Glory be, she accepted. We arranged to take the train to East St. Louis for Danny to meet my family. I had already had a telegram from my father, welcoming Danny into the family, so he clearly understood that my mind was made up! I had asked for my parents to be at home to receive a telephone call in which I told them of my plans to propose. The house at 1728 North 48th was very small.

Danny slept in the north bedroom. I slept on a cot in the dining room.

The next day we went to a jeweler's in St. Louis with my mother's diamond. We got it mounted in a ring that Danny continues to wear to this day in 2009.

We were married in December 1943 in Washington D.C. in the beautiful All Souls Unitarian Church on 16th street by Reverend Jim Flint, whom Danny had known for many years. Without question, marrying Danny was the best decision I have ever made. Danny has most graciously accepted my foibles, idiosyncrasies and quirks.

Our wedding 1943

Danny's sister, Mino, was the maid of honor and her older brother, Farrington Jr. was the best man. Both sets of parents were able to attend the wedding. Two of Danny's best friends came from New York for the occasion. The time was set at 6:00 PM on Saturday, so people from both our offices could come, and quite a few of them did.

I took just three days off work to have a kind of a honeymoon. I felt I was needed for the war work. In our three day honeymoon, we moved into our new apartment. We needed a book shelf and so we took the bus to a lumber yard, to buy some boards with

Moving into our Arlington Apartment after our wedding.

which to make a brick and board book case. We were walking about a mile and a half back to the apartment, carrying three four foot boards. A passerby saw us and stopped and offered to give us a ride. Turns out, he was a carpenter and was interested in our project. I was in uniform and perhaps he was also showing a kindness to a serviceman.

After VE Day I was sent out of Washington and I was stationed in Philadelphia, inspecting personnel offices for compliance with the Services of Supply regulations. Danny remained in Washington where she was working at the Department of Agriculture. The war continued in the Pacific, and all we knew at the time was that the atom bombs had been dropped and had wrought utter devastation, but we were sure the bombs would end the war. The dismay over the horror of the bombs only came later. Danny's father, who had been working on the bombs in Chicago, polled the staff members as regards their opinions of the dropping of the bomb. He said after the bombs were dropped, "I think they have saved our sons, but I'm not so sure about our grandsons."

I was in Philadelphia on VJ Day and went back to Washington to visit Danny on that weekend when there was jubilation all over.

Back at Princeton 1946

I had left Princeton as a first year graduate student living at the graduate college way out on the hill away from the university main campus in 1941. I returned as a married graduate student and instructor in January 1946.

On our return, I found Princeton with a shortage of housing for married graduate students. I walked up and down the streets searching for an empty house, and I found one at 29 Chestnut Street. After an inquiry to a neighbor, I learned it was owned by Miss Julia Foley who lived several blocks away.

I put on my army uniform and my most persuasive mood to go talk to Miss Foley. She agreed to rent the house for, as I remember, $30 a month with it being understood that I would move her furniture to the second floor bedroom. I was free to paint the walls. Miss Foley had been a maid in the Woodrow Wilson Princeton Household.

The house at 29 Chestnut was technically "modern" in that it had inside plumbing. But it had no central heat. There was a hole in the floor for heat to rise up from a stove in the kitchen to give a little heat to our bedroom above. There was a stool in the bathroom upstairs but there was only a large black cast iron tub in the kitchen where we took our baths in water heated on the stove. In Princeton they sold and used hard coal. While I was quite familiar with burning soft coal, I found it difficult to keep the stove burning through the night with the hard coal. There was no refrigeration in the house. Miss Foley had merely put food in a big kettle and lowered the kettle into a cistern to try to keep things a little cooler.

Refrigerators were not made during the war so people who wanted to buy one put their names on a list and had to wait their turn, as new ones gradually came into the retail stores. We were afraid that the pressure from local permanent residents might take precedence over a request from a student who expected to be only a short time in town. Fortunately for us, the store manager went strictly down his list and we felt fortunate to be able to buy a refrigerator.

Later we were the first to move into 218A Marshall--Princeton's new married student housing, several blocks away from the main campus. We had several visitors here and I remember Aunt Lillian visited us there once in order to take an all day excursion to New York City. Danny and Aunt Lillian went to see the Rockettes. We were young and adjustable then. We bought used bikes and got by very well for several months, until we moved to Lawrence.

PART 3

Career

University of Kansas

In 1947 we moved from Princeton, New Jersey to 4F Sunnyside in Lawrence, Kansas. I was employed by the University of Kansas as an instructor, with the promise of being promoted when I earned my Ph.D. degree.

Subsequently, I was promoted through the ranks to full Professor and in 1989, when I reached age 70, I became a Professor Emeritus.

Danny and me in Lawrence

When we arrived in Lawrence, it had very re-

cently grown to be a first class city legally. This meant it had 15,000 people. In 2009 it has about 90,000. The growth of the university explains the growth of Lawrence. With the population in Douglas County of perhaps 100,000 it well may be one of the fastest growing cities in the state and maybe in the nation. In a nationwide survey, KU has been rated high as a "best buy" among state universities.

Professor Emeritus

Upon our arrival in Lawrence I became part of the Political Science Department. I taught a course in Township Government. It was new for me and I had to keep ahead of the students. I soon dropped Township Government since as the government structure changed, the course became obsolete. I moved into the teaching of Public Personnel Administration and Municipal Finance, both in Lawrence and in our Johnson County outreach campus.

Our faculty was always somewhat divided on the issue of which was more important: teaching or research. Those favoring research tended to be more interested in trying to make clones of themselves by encouraging students to do research. Counter wise, those interested in teaching tend to be more interested in making teachers.

As my colleague, Professor Edwin O. Stene got more involved in training City Managers (KUCMAT), I inherited the management of the Interdepartmental Personnel Administration Program. The title of this program was later changed to Human Resource Management. As a major component it required students to have internships -- a concept I strongly endorse. For many years, the university also had me offer a course in Human Resource Management in Kansas City. This program also required students to intern in the summer between their Junior and Senior years. Some students so impressed their managers that they were employed after graduation. Once a month on Tuesdays, I would take a car load of students to the meetings of the Personnel Officers Association of the Greater Kansas City area.

In the thirty years that I taught in this program, I typically had 500 students each year, so I taught about 15,000 students. If we assume a median salary for a Human Resource Director to be $100,000 per year, the ball park estimate would be that my students and I contributed around a billion and a half to our GNP. This was a very successful program, but times changed and the Business School figured the program should be theirs only. The Dean did not like this course, as he thought it was too easy, and it was hard to get people to teach in interdepartmental programs, so the major was discontinued.

Measured in another way, I might have influenced at least one Governor (Bennett), and one U.S. senator (Nancy Landon Kassebaum), since they were students of mine. Additionally, hopefully, there are several thousand of my students who are more knowledgeable and presumably better citizens as a result of being my students. My students dispersed far and wide so that I even found myself being lectured by a former student while attending an Interhostel trip in Holland.

I should note that I had only one teaching job in my life. My department at KU treated us well. I got a leave of absence when I wanted one. I got leave for six consecutive years to be Director of the Legislative Research Department.

When we arrived in Lawrence we lived in a Sunnyside apartment and from the bottom of the hill, I could wait for the whistle to blow, signaling that classes were out and there were ten minutes before the next class would start. This meant I had *ten* minutes to get to class on the fourth floor of Snow Hall and not be too out of breath to start to lecture. I was 28 years old. I doubt I could do this in thirty minutes today. The spot where our apartment was has now become a parking lot on the east part of the campus.

During the second year of us living in Sunnyside, our son Jon, was born. Our apartment was on the second floor, with a very small back balcony. Immediately below the balcony were the garbage cans. We

Me with my first child, Jonathan Daniels Drury

would walk down the stairs and deposit our household trash there. One day our good friend, Ann Chernick, just happened to be at the garbage cans and looked up in time to hold out her arms and catch our young son Jonathan, who had fallen from the balcony. Thus he was saved from possible serious harm or even death. Within twenty four hours I had secured chicken fencing to the balcony so this could not happen again!

In 1948 we purchased the lot at 1648 Mississippi and had an architect design a simple Cape Cod house. But in the end we decided it was too costly, and selected a pre-assembled house, which came in sections. We had a crew assemble the house on site. Can you believe we paid $1600 for the lot so close to the university? I wonder what such a lot would be worth today.

1648 Mississippi Street

When we took our trip to Japan, we rented 1648 Mississippi to Cliff and Lee Ketzel. In 1958 we sold the 1648 Mississippi Street house and moved to Fifteenth Street.

We stayed at KU because we liked Lawrence - the location, our housing and our friends. We liked the freedom of having vacation times on a university schedule.

The Student Union at KU was set on fire in the 1960s when there was a lot of unrest about the war in Vietnam on campuses across the country. I was working in Topeka at the Kansas Legislative Research Department at that time, and heard that the National Guard was called out to quell the riots. When I returned to teaching in 1976, after my time in the KLRD, I found students much less docile than I remembered them being before I left. I found that since the 60s, students have become less respectful toward their professors and a different kind of relationship between students and professors has developed. Students and professors now go by first names and professors are no longer viewed as being on a pedestal. There is more personal interaction and a lot more discussion between professors and students in the classroom today. I felt more comfortable giving lectures than facilitating discussions. In retrospect I think perhaps I lectured too much. I developed a technique, equivalent in a primitive way, to the modern power point presentation outline slide. It was my practice to be at the door of a lecture hall when the bell rang to dismiss the previous class. I would then have ten minutes to put a somewhat detailed outline of what I was going to talk about on the black board.

Today I would feel comfortable in teaching courses in public finance. For me the central ideas in public and personal budgeting are itemization, comparison, and justification. I mainly taught undergraduate courses in Lawrence. Sometimes I taught graduate courses in Finance and Human Resource Management.

The KU College of Liberal Arts and Sciences almost requires members to write a book to be promoted to Full Professor. I conformed and my book, *The Government of Kansas* went through five editions, partly because the training unit in the State Human Resource Department ruled that every supervisor in the State Government should know something about the workings of the other parts of the government of the state.

Professor Ethan P. Allen

Professor Ethan P. Allen was the chair of the Political Science Department at the University of Kansas. As chair, he was my boss. He assigned me to be in charge of editing *Your Government* – a four page monthly publication which was released during the school year with bulk mailing to high school students to inform them about Kansas State Government. I was in charge of this project for several years. It was sponsored by KU, as an outreach to high school students in the state.

Part of his job was to decide how much of the "raise money" allotted by the college, each faculty member would get each year. Some of the time of his chairmanship, there was an advisory committee to make recommendations to him. I served on this advisory committee under a later Chairman. I found myself in a position of having to judge between my close compatriots, which was difficult.

Ethan came to KU with a broad program for the department and the Governmental Research Center. He employed Ray Carman and Vernon Koch as advisors to be on call for any local government official to solve local government problems. Ethan had for me, some of the attributes of a father figure.

The Department had monthly meetings at various places such as the Castle Tea Room in Lawrence and the Sirloin Restaurant in North Lawrence. In general the department was closely knit and there was a sense of camaraderie at these meetings. At one time there was a fraction of the department that felt that the chairman had not pushed the administration hard enough for salary increases. At least three of the professors joined in a team, without the chairman's approval, to get an audience with the dean in order to air their disappointments.

The Dean of the college, Dean Lawson had brought Ethan in to chair the Department immediately after the war. I came to Kansas after being recommended by Professor George Graham who worked with Ethan in the Budget Division in the war. I was glad to have this contact, as Affirmative Action was just on the horizon and that required a wide search and a much larger pool of applicants to fill a post like the one I got.

Kansas Legislative Research Department

Frederic Guild was head of the Kansas Legislative Research Department (KLRD) when I worked there during summers in the 1950s. He had a most distinguished career in his association with legislatures in a number of states. He was a hard worker, an innovator, and a dynamic force in several states, but most importantly, in his home state of Kansas. I remember that most of the time, he had a partly smoked cigar in his mouth.

Fred knew there were never enough students in KU summer sessions to let every teacher in our Political Science Department teach. He knew we liked to have summer jobs. So he would offer us jobs for two months in the summer, working for KLRD. I worked in Topeka with Fred for at least three summers along with Bill Cape and Cliff Ketzel (who taught courses in American Foreign Policy and subjects far afield from Kansas Government).

Fred (and possibly others unknown to me) persuaded the Legislative Leadership to arrange for Interim Legislative Committees during the summer to study subjects and draft legislation to introduce when the whole legislature reconvened. Sessions could then get off to a quicker start.

For reasons I do not know, the Lieutenant Governor decided Fred Guild should be fired. I remember quite well when the Chairman of the Legislative Council called me to come for an interview for the Directorship. I made a trip to privately ask Richard Ryan, the number two man in the KLRD office, if he wanted the Directorship. He assured me that he did not. I was appointed Director of the KLDR and served for seven years.

Richard (Dick) Ryan (from KLRD) and Jim Bibb (from the Governor's office) knew more about Kansas finances than anyone in the state. As soon as Robert Bennett became governor he had a private telephone installed so that he could call and get immediate information and advice from Dick.

For a number of years previously, Jim Bibb as Budget Director, had operated as the "Fiscal Governor of the State." He used a system that enhanced his control, but was questionable. Bibb and his staff prepared evaluative studies for the Governor. These studies were included in the Governor's Budget and were sent to the Legislature. Then when the session began, each of the analysts from the Governor's Budget Division shifted their roles and began working for the Legislature. At that point, they were working on an adoption of what they had earlier prepared. They could thus not independently and objectively review what they themselves had so recently prepared.

When Bennett was governor he set up the system of having a fiscal officer, Marlin Rein.

I employed Marlin Rein to be the head of a budget section in the KLRD. This group prepared independently their own studies of state agencies resulting in a volume the size of five Topeka telephone directories. This gave the legislators on the appropriation subcommittees better information to question the agency heads. They could now use studies done by the legislative staff.

Marlin Rein later was lured over to the KU Medical Center where he served as their Legislative Public Relations Man (a fancy way of describing their "Lobbyist").

I had an interesting relationship with a lobbyist, John Keith, representing the American Trucker's Association. At that time, the American Trucking Association was strongly opposed to the "ton mile tax" in Kansas. This tax caused the truckers to keep records that they found expensive. While they doubtless would have liked to have had the tax repealed, they would benefit from not having the tax based on the number of tons a carrier moved. If the legislature would agree to discontinue the "ton mile tax" they would have less objection to the tax. Keith was a persuasive man and he got his way.

In 1976 I decided I had to choose between my teaching career and continuing to be KLRD Director which would mean a permanent move to Topeka. I was very doubtful if I could handle the "politics" of keeping my job of Director when the Legislative leadership changed. Earl Nehring was chair of the KU Department and would set my salary with consideration for my seven years of leave without pay. I decided to play it safe, possibly too safe, since at that time the legislative leader did not have any personal staff. Now that both majority and minority leaders have staff, the Director would be safe from politics.

Identifying with Political Parties

Over the years my views have changed on whether I should inform or not inform my students and others about how I voted in partisan elections. When I applied for the Directorship of the Legislative Research Department I was happy that my position has been not to make my personal politics known. On the other hand, I think that after talking social problems and government with someone for an hour, they would classify me as an Independent-leaning Democrat.

I doubt that there was any uniformity among our teaching staff as to how to handle this element of their teaching in the Political Science Department. I have the general impression however that the Department faculty was perceived as mostly Democrats with the exception of Roy Laird, who at one point was the faculty adviser to the Young Republican Club, and Earl Nehring who is a registered Republican.

PART 4:

Leaves from KU

Japan 1954-1955

At the end of World War II, the Armed Services had huge amounts of military equipment in Japan and elsewhere overseas. It would be costly to ship it home and the manufacturers of the equipment were interested only in developing new and improved equipment. Senator Fulbright got an idea and sold Congress on it: Each country was allowed to buy the equipment with their local currency, not dollars. This money would be available as grants for students and scholars like me to work or study abroad in these countries.

I was realistic enough to know that with only my native English language, I would never get a Fulbright Professorship to Western Europe where it was required that one teach in the *lingua franca*. So I applied to go to Japan, since I could teach in English there, and was accepted. This became our first experience living in a foreign country.

By chance when my appointment was announced in our local newspaper, some acquaintances invited us to come and meet their friend, Kate Hansen, who was a missionary in Sendai. She lived in Sendai, but was visiting the States at that time. Kate told us of Carl and Eddie Sipple, who became very good friends, confidants, advisors, and coaches. They were missionaries who taught at Miyagi Girls College which is adjacent to Tohoku University in Sendai.

The Fulbright Commission paid for our passage to Japan on the only passenger ship Japan had. It had been refurbished from its war time service. The ventilation in the stateroom was poor and so while on board, I laid out my next days' clothes at night, slipped into them as quickly as I could and got to the deck and fresh air, every morning.

It was September and our northerly route was very rough -- so rough that one morning, we found the waves had sufficient force to break the glass in the Pilot house, many feet above the water. It was so rough that the Captain was concerned when he saw us walking little two year old Jane on the open deck and cautioned us to watch her closely.

Upon our arrival in Sendai, it was through the Sipples that we met Akiho-san. Imagine our surprise when we went with Carl to see Akiho-san and negotiate with her about working for us. Carl, a tall slim man over six feet, got down on the tatami (straw mat) on his knees and bowed his head to the floor in the traditional Japanese greeting. She agreed to become our cook and general household manager. Her English was somewhat limited. I don't remember what we agreed to pay her for being our cook for six days a week. After the war, she had been the sole wage earner in the Akiho family and had worked as a cook for an American army family. She knew American style cooking. It was only in later days there, that we learned she was skilled in Chinese cooking as well.

Akiho-san found for us Koide-san to be her assistant and primarily wash our clothes by hand. She had lived with her husband in Canada. He was the gardener of the Japanese Embassy in Toronto. I must explain we lived in a small Japanese house that had a most unusual wooden bath tub. The wooden tub in the kitchen had a big metal container built into it and in this, a fire was used to heat the water which we used for our baths. The tub was in the wall between the bathroom and the kitchen. In the bathroom we would stand on wooden slats over the drain, soap ourselves and then pour water over ourselves with a ladle to rinse off. Then we would get into the tub and soak and get warm.

Jon and Jane in the
soaking tub

All family members used the same soaking water. The next morning Koide-san would use the water to wash our clothes.

When Koide-san bought chicken for us, the meat was taken off the bones, which were packaged up with the meat and were used to boil up for chicken broth. Koide-san  asked us if she could take the bones home to boil them a second time to make broth for her family, as she had done in the war. I question if she would get much nourishment from a second boiling of the chicken bones.

Our house had been rented for us by the university. By American standards it was very small, but we adjusted. We had a small entrance-way where people took off their shoes (to save wear

Danny - Japanese Style

on the tatami) and then a twelve-mat room which served as the sleeping room, dining room and living room. A mat is approximately three feet by six feet. Thus we had a 216 foot room to do most of our living in. We each had a thick futon mattress to sleep on, on the relatively soft tatami floor. The futons were rolled up and stored in the cupboard in the daytime, when the room was furnished with pillows to sit on and a short legged table, like a coffee table. This room had an inset which was called the toka-noma where a decorative scroll was displayed. The rooms were arranged so that we had a four foot wide porch on the South that allowed the sun to come in and warm us up.

About four PM as the sun started to go down, we could hear our neighbors closing wooden doors. Then we would start running our wooden doors along a track to protect us from the worst of the cold. Lots were very small and arranged so that the longer dimension was running east and west so that the house could have the southern exposure

Me skiing in Japan

to more of the sunlight. The building code required that there be opaque windows on the north side of the house for privacy.

While in Japan, we were able to do some travelling around. We spent a week in Kyoto in cherry blossom season. On one of our trips we bought a little model of a traditional Japanese house, which can be taken apart piece by piece so the inside of each room can be seen, including fine details such as the tatami mats.

Our whole family went to a ski resort in early winter in Japan. Our room was heated with a charcoal burning stove, covered by wire in the center of the room. Our futons were placed so that each member of the Drury family had his or her feet pointed at the heater, and we wrapped our feet in blankets and placed them on top of the wire covering the stove to keep them warm.

We enjoyed our first encounter as described above sufficiently, that we went back at the end of the season and we were disappointed to find no snow and much charcoal ash!

We also took several sightseeing day trips from Sendai, among them trips to view the maple leaves in the fall and to visit a silk factory.

I taught Political Science at Tohoku University in Sendai. It was one of the Imperial provincial universities in a city of half a million people. Japan followed the German pattern of assigning the discipline of Political Science to the Law School. I taught a course in American Government in the Law School. I often had lunch with instructors at the university and found that the man who was teaching Western History did not have anything about American History in his program, so I volunteered to give a lecture on American History. When I got back to Lawrence, I was talking to the Chairman of the KU History Department and jokingly offered to help out whenever he or some of his colleagues had trouble covering all of American History, for I had developed a way to do it in fifty minutes!

The U.S. Department of State operated an American Culture Center several miles from the university. I suspect that there may have been more books in English in the Culture Center library than there were in the Tohoku University library. I will never know whether the students in their black uniforms came to the Center because of the books or because of the nice warmth in the Center, which was unlike any other Japanese building.

In 1954, I was one of five college professors at Tohoko University, (but the only native English speaker) who were given the responsibility of selecting candidates to come to the United States to study at Michigan State University. Michigan State was the university that specialized in teaching English as a second language. There were forty applicants.

I was amused many times when the Japanese professors would ask "How did you come to pick *up* Michigan University?" rather than "pick *out* Michigan State University," as a native speaker would say.

I noted numerous differences between Japanese universities and American universities. From my perspective, the librarian at Tohoku University viewed his job as keeping the books in the library and did not to encourage their use. I also noted that the professors considered themselves more in charge of the university than the professors in the States do. Japanese professors had a greater say in who became the president of the university. Sometimes the Japanese professors would consider it better to lecture at a university other than where they were employed, probably so they could draw two pay checks.

I soon realized that my students were more interested in hearing my English than learning about American Government. I assigned a term paper and a student handed me a 12 page report. I read it. It was good, bordering on excellent. I could not have written it myself without much effort and several drafts. I went to the Culture Center and looked at several of the standard American text books. In a very short time I found the chapter that my student had copied and handed in as his assignment. I checked out the book and took it to my office to show the student why I could not accept the term paper and give him credit. Credit belonged to the author of the text book from which he had copied. I think I managed to convey to the student that this was the wrong thing to do. He had not understood that one could not merely copy another author's work.

At the University in Sendai, a fluent English speaking Professor, Shigeru Oda in the Law School, was assigned to be my mentor and contact in the university. Most days Oda would telephone a local shop and order us bowls of various flavored rice which were delivered by a boy on a bicycle. Bicycles were much used in Japan as a means of transport. I, in fact, got so adept at moving around on a bicycle in Japan that I could ride it while carrying my brief case and holding an umbrella! Oda became my mentor, counselor, and friend. Later Oda became a long serving Justice in the International Course of Justice in The Hague. He has written more opinions for the Court than any other Justice. Fortunately our paths have crossed several times. Just by chance, we met several times in different parts of the world. He returned some summers to Japan for medical checkups.

The Director of the American Culture Center was Lynn Few. We got to know him and his wife, Ellen, who was unfortunately a semi-invalid, as a result of polio. On our way back home from Sendai, we visited them in Rome, where Lynn's next assignment was.

I remember being on the stage in a big auditorium, in Japan, with Lynn, describing how we take baths so differently in the U.S. than the Japanese do. For many Japanese, the time in the bath is the *only* time in the whole day when they are warm. I recall clearly, being with a group of male friends, visiting in a Japanese Inn, where there was no central heat. In the course of the evening we went twice to the bath to warm up and then we went back to our room for further sociability.

Me and Lynn Few on the right

Fortuitously, 1955 was the year Danny's father was President of the American Chemical Society and was making a world tour of Universities. When he was in Tokyo, we went down for his dinner meeting. (Akiho-san babysat our two children.) On our way back to Sendai, a friendly Tohoku Chemistry professor arranged for a brief tour of Nikko - a famous Japanese Shrine. In Japan they have a saying: "One should not say anything is beautiful until one has seen Nikko." The famous carving of the monkeys that see, speak and hear no evil, is at Nikko.

We did not know of the Japanese custom of seeing people off at the railroad station. We were chagrined to learn that quite a crowd had assembled at 9:00 PM to see Professor Daniels off to Tokyo. (Mother Daniels stayed with us for several more weeks and returned to the U.S. on her own.)

When it came to our own departure we knew what to look for. The President of the university honored me by coming to the station, and as our train pulled away, waiting patiently forty or fifty feet away were our good friends, the Sipples to wave us goodbye.

I was in a cemetery in Japan where American missionaries were buried. With me was a Japanese teaching colleague who was a Buddhist. He noticed how missionaries of differing denominations were buried in separate plots. He asked, "Were the Christians so divided in their beliefs that they wanted their remains to be buried next to their own type of Christian?" I explained that it was not the case at all. Each of the various sects of Christians had their own plots because they had the responsibility to bury their own missionaries.

531 Days in Pakistan – February, 1961 – August, 1962

In the fall of 1960, my 202 friend Dave Brown called me and asked if I was interested in going to Pakistan as a contract employee of the University of Southern California (USC) under the sponsorship of the U.S. Agency for International Development. My job would be to set up a Department of Public Administration at the University of the Punjab at Lahore, West Pakistan. I checked with Ethan Allen, the Chairman of our department, and found I could get a leave of absence.

I telephoned Danny's cousin, Dave Bell, who had been to India on some kind of consulting, and got a generally favorable report of what little he knew of this sort of AID program. So I decided to say I would go, if appointed.

At Thanksgiving time, we were in St. Louis and an interview was arranged for me. The USC Chief of the Party, Dean Emory Olsen, was told of my interest and arranged to "interview" me as his plane stopped briefly in St. Louis. Candidly it was more of a pep talk for me to sign on rather than a job interview.

USC offered me a contract. Under the then-current U.S. income tax law, if a citizen were out of the country for 531 days, he or she did not have to pay U.S. income tax. (This meant I got about a 25% increase in salary).

USC arranged for a meeting in Los Angeles of about fifteen people whom they had recruited to go to Pakistan. We met at a building close to the university a number of times between Christmas and New Years. There were several "short termers" who were mostly U.S. government specialists in their field, and were to come for periods of about five weeks. They were able to leave their jobs for only that long. Then there were "long termers" whose stay was to be 531 days. USC was to establish four Departments of Public Administration - one in Karachi, one in Lahore, one in Dacca (then the capital of East Pakistan,) and one to be moved to the new capital when it was established at Islamabad. Each department was to have a library. The Department of Public Administration to be established at the university of the Punjab in Lahore was to be my particular responsibility.

Numerous training programs were begun at the four institutes, with the long-termers and the short-termers providing the faculty. As far as the university programs were concerned, Pakistani students were to be sent to USC to get Ph.D.'s in Public Administration. It was a broadly conceived program with many parts, aimed at trying to "jump start" the new nation of Pakistan into the twentieth century. The nation of Pakistan was created in 1947 and had no real bureaucratic tradition, the way India did, because under British rule most of the civil servants had been Hindus and at the time of partition Hindus moved to India, even though their homes had been in the area that became Pakistan. Partition came about when the British Colonists gave over control to the local population, and Pakistan (with two non-contiguous parts) and India became two separate nations. About a million people lost their lives in the ensuing conflict.

We arranged for a four-week itinerary of sight-seeing before we got to Pakistan. It was our second major foreign trip - the first being to Japan in 1954. We had stops in Lisbon, Madrid, Nice, Athens, Beirut, and Istanbul. We had problems with weather and airline strikes. Though we had a few trying travel incidents, they were soon forgotten. We found it quite possible to travel with three children under fourteen years of age.

The U.S. government provided us with a house, Army Post Office privileges, and State Department commissary privileges.

We were assigned to the house at 21Q Gulbarg, a section of Lahore, about twenty minutes by car from downtown Lahore.

Under USAID rules we were entitled to three bedrooms, with air conditioners provided for each bedroom. The bedrooms were large. When it was hot, we had our meals served in our bedroom.

As soon as we arrived, men, and generally men only, came to our door seeking employment. They came with their reference letters from past employers and somehow we were to learn of their qualifications such as honesty, loyalty, cooking ability, and above all else their physical health. We had each of the job seekers that we seriously considered go to the local Christian Hospital and we paid for their physical exams. We settled on Hussain. He brought with him Abdul, who was from his village and who knew much less English than Hussain. When others in our little community of USAID compatriots told of firing of the servants, we were glad to have Hussain and Abdul. Clearly Hussain was the chief cook and in charge. As he put it, Hussain took care of Sahib – what he called me - the head of the household - and Sahib took care of Hussain and the others. We came to learn this meant paying for trips to the health clinic and in cold weather, buying warm second-hand overcoats and blankets for the servants.

Next came the Dhobi - a laundry man - who came three days a week to wash and iron our clothes. Then there was the woman "sweeper." She was the lowliest of the low, in their somewhat recognized caste system. Abdul would clean our bathroom, but the sweeper cleaned the servants' toilet which was in the servants' quarters in the back yard.

We adjusted to a new way of life. Mem-sahib, (Danny) the manager of the house, was the "boss lady" and directed the work of two full-time live-in servants and many part time servants. One of the full time servants, who did not live in, was a full-time gardener who took care of our 150 by 200 foot yard, which was on two levels. When the monsoons came we were prepared. The front and back yards had sunken areas to collect the monsoon rains and prevent the house from flooding. The sunken sections in the yards became pools with two and a half feet of water, which

would soon evaporate once the monsoons were over. On the upper level one did not even try to grow flowers - it was just too hot.
But we almost always had some kind of flowers in bloom in pots
along the driveway.

21Q Gulbarg was a big rambling two-story structure typical
of the houses there - clearly upper class housing. It was brick and
masonry construction with an effort to get as much cross ventilation as possible. Partially up the stairway to the roof there was a
small room, which despite its location was called the "Go Down"
- the British term for a store room. It was here that Hussain and
Danny kept food supplies with records to show that the servants
did not steal any of our food. Then a few steps higher, was the
flat roof. Part of this area had a cover for protection from the sun.
Many Pakistanis slept on this area of the roof in hot weather,
in their movable cots called *charpoys*. This was also where the
women of the house could get a breath of fresh air and hopefully
a cooling breeze in privacy, as they were not meant to be seen in
public at all.

There were others on the payroll of the USAID mission. We
had a "chukadar" (night watchman) who came each night to protect us from robbers and malcontents. He walked around our
house off and on each night occasionally coughing - we came to
think he did that to let us know he was there.

One morning I awoke to hear our nine year old daughter,
Jane, yelling, "It's morning, it's morning!" I could not understand
why she was so excited about the morning. I ran to see, wearing
barely any clothes. In fact, she was yelling, "It's burning, it's burning!" The air conditioner wires had caught fire due to overheating.
I grabbed hold of the plug and pulled it out from the socket. That
put the fire out. No serious harm was done.

Our USC group was assigned a big American station wagon
with a driver, Hashmi, who picked us up each day and drove us
about as needed. Hashmi worked hard to get me to let him carry
my briefcase. His culture had no place for Sahib to carry his own
briefcase.

There were still others to take care of the "helpless" Americans. We were told that when water left the water plant in Lahore it was quite safe to drink, but there were so many leaks and breaks in the water lines that it was not safe when it reached the houses. Moreover the supply was uncertain. So a USAID truck came once a week to fill our water tank, which was on the roof of our two-story house. Additionally, we boiled all water that we drank.

To set up a Department of Public Administration at the University of the Punjab, most of the contacts at the university were with Mian Bashir. Unfortunately for me, Mian Bashir had been educated in Britain and really preferred their educational system. To the extent I could, I worked with Shah Sab, the treasurer of the university.

They found me an office, in their downtown old campus. I drafted regulations officially establishing a Department. Later we selected candidates to go to the Los Angeles Campus for their Ph.D.'s and return as the teaching staff. I did little teaching myself, but depended on others to do teaching. I have the impression that the Pakistanis are generally not as "haughty" as some of the Hindu Indians I have met.

Things moved slowly--disappointingly slowly, but before I left, the department was officially established. As a "stand alone" project I got the money to hold a two-day program on Public Administration for young Pakistani teachers at other universities.

A Pakistani who had a Ph.D. in public administration from Syracuse University was appointed as the dean of the new school. In 2009 the department was redirected to include Private Business.

I was able to go to Dacca on three occasions and see some of that country and what was going on with our program there. Professor Don Hecock, from Wayne University, was in charge of setting up the Department of Public Administration at the University of Dacca. In general, the University of the Punjab had more of a physical plant and was more established than the University of Dacca.

Lahore

In 1961 when we were living in Lahore, West Pakistan we, along with hundreds of others, including Jackie Kennedy went to see the Horse Show. There were so many members of the press for the event that the U.S. Embassy "commandeered" the big Ford Station Wagon and driver, Hashmi, normally assigned to us. Jackie, known for her interest in horses, was the object of much interest from the locals. They lined the streets of her reported route to catch a glimpse of her, only to be disappointed. The next morning, when she left Lahore, she took an unexpected horse ride and was two hours off her schedule, so again the crowds lining the route could not catch a glimpse of her. The airport had been closed down for her security and planes were much delayed.

I took a trip out from Lahore to the rural areas. In colonial days, the British had set up districts into which they sent a government official to hold court. The local officers would hold court and allow anyone who wanted to come and complain about any matter, to do so. In each of the districts there was a rest house where passing officials could rest and eat. The Pakistanis had continued the system. There was a local attendant at these rest houses who knew how to prepare one meal--that was chicken curry rice. We got our food and board on this trip at these district houses. I arranged to go on tour with one of the local officers, as he went to have hearings and resolve complaints. On that tour, I slept on a bed in one of these rest houses, with a boy six feet above me, in the gable of the room, pulling a string back and forth all night long to move the fan to keep me cool.

Hunza

Explorer off to Hunza

Dave Brown knew that the Mir of Hunza would be at the Horse Show in Lahore, as well as other important people like the Khan of Karat and the Wally of Swat. All three of these were "rulers" of their separate little isolated valleys. Each represented the central government in their areas and exercised some governmental powers, especially in the adjudication of conflicting claims to water for irrigation. Dave visited with the Mir at the horse show and got us an invitation to come to Hunza to see the Mir there.

We were a party of eight, travelling to Hunza; Dave Brown, his son Christopher, me, our son Jon, and four others. We went on a twenty-passenger aircraft in turbulent air, with one of the passengers vomiting for the entire duration of the flight. The airport in Hunza was very primitive and had a short landing strip, but we made it. When we landed, we soon learned of two nurses that were in the area, who had set out to walk around the world, starting at the World Fair in Brussels several years earlier. They had worked at local hospitals whenever they ran out of money. They were completely unaware of the danger of weather changes and freezing conditions at that altitude in the Hindu Kush Mountains and they were about to walk across the UN cease fire line that was keeping peace between India and Pakistan in their dispute over the ownership of Kashmir.

We were invited to a tea with the local representative of the government. This government representative had heard of the two nurses and he informed his superiors. They instructed him to arrest the nurses and send them to Islamabad to be deported. This actually would help them, for in several hours they would cover hundreds of miles which they otherwise would have had to walk, as they progressed around the world.

Hunza was the setting for a novel, "Lost Horizon," by Hilton. It is an isolated area where people were reputed to live longer than elsewhere in the world. It was reputed to be a land of eternal youth. There was speculation as to why. Was it the water? *Pani* is the Urdu word for water. Hunza Pani was a pleasant tasting sweet wine. It turned out that the local mullah had ruled that even Muslims who could not drink alcohol were permitted to drink "Hunza Pani." Hunza is a very rocky mountainous place near K2, with limited greenery. Only in the valleys are there terraced fields in which rice is grown.

We met a lady named Bertha and her red-headed son at the airport in Hunza. She had divorced her husband and was in Hunza because she felt her son should have some adventure in his life. The number of jeeps for hire was smaller than expected, as some of the jeeps were being used to fight a locust plague. We joined in a loose agreement with Bertha that we would share a jeep for the rest of the trip into Hunza. The road was a primitive, completely unpaved sandy road – little more than a path up the rocky, mountainous terrain, remote from anywhere. There were many horseshoe turns. Many of the turns were so tight that even a Jeep could not make the turn unassisted. One of the drivers would get out of the jeep and set the stone enabling the driver to complete his turn. On one occasion I picked up a fair sized stone and threw it down to the river. I saw it splash into the river fifteen seconds later, suggesting that the river was many hundred feet below. We felt that the circumstances were such that members of the family should be in different jeeps in case one jeep fell over the edge.

We proceeded at ten or fifteen miles an hour until we came to a place where the road was too narrow for the jeep to go. A repair crew was rebuilding the road. One man with a rope tied around his body went over the side and was let down gradually until he was able to find a good solid rock on which to start rebuilding the road. He would search out other solid rocks and gradually add rocks one at a time, cantilevering the foundation out, until the

road was wide enough for a jeep to pass on. We were delayed several hours while the road was rebuilt.

The Adventurer   The treacherous road in Hunza

Two Summers in Costa Rica

In 1965, we were part of a two year exchange program with the University of Costa Rica, funded by a Carnegie Grant to KU. We had Spanish lessons in Lawrence for a month and then flew to Costa Rica for the rest of the summer. The group of families participating in the program developed a sense of camaraderie and we participated in many activities together. The five in our family often joined with seven in the Mills family and a few others, and on many Sundays we rented a small bus for trips around the San Jose area. We lived in a high rise hotel in downtown San Jose.

In the next summer, (1966) we and several families drove to Costa Rica. We drove from Kansas and traveled approximately three thousand miles in the same time zone. The Pan-American highway was a two lane road that took us through Mexico and Central America. There were mountainous regions and in many places the travel was slow-going. Because we had been warned that people occasionally slept along the roadside at night, we wanted to be in our hotels well before dark each day. Additionally, we had to time ourselves in order to avoid reaching the borders during the two hour shut-downs for siesta each afternoon. We needed to keep a constant eye on the gas gauge as gas stations were sometimes far apart. We also had to keep an adequate supply of drinking water with us.

I had just completed my book, *The Government of Kansas* when we first went to Costa Rica. When I learned there was no comparable volume about Costa Rican government, I took on the project of recruiting various authors to write chapters in order to compile such a book. Although I found someone in San Jose who agreed to coordinate the project, it never materialized. One of the weaknesses of the university system there was their refusal to pay salaries for full time professors. Instead, the universities hired adjuncts to teach part time. This meant that many of my contacts who had agreed to do the writing were actually more interested in other pursuits besides academic ones.

In our second summer in Costa Rica we rented a small house and the children attended local schools. On the weekends we explored and made excursions into the beautiful, green, fertile country.

I was able to arrange what turned out to be one of the most unusual travels of my life. It was a tour of Don Luis Wachong's *finca* (farm) which is in southern Costa Rica close to the border of Panama.

Our little cluster of KU professors got to know Don Luis Wachong through his son and daughter who had both been students at the University of Kansas. Don Luis Wachong was an overseas Chinese millionaire with many holdings in Costa Rica. I knew he had a base in San Jose, the capital of Costa Rica; an establishment in Golfito - a banana port on the Southern Pacific West Coast of Costa Rica; and a substantial *finca* in the mountains of Southern Costa Rica. He invited me to see his *finca*.

At 8:00 in the morning I met Don Luis Wachong in San Jose, and as it turned out others too, to make the trip to his farm-- *finca*. We had one four-door typical American car and set off for the *finca*. The road to Golfito was a normal two lane asphalt road going through the fertile green hillside of Costa Rica. The highway south from San Jose was part of the Pan American highway and was a good road, and the talk was pleasant.

With us was a fellow named Sam, who was a retired U.S. government agriculture employee. He had been stationed in San Jose, liked it, and decided to retire there. He bought a *finca* immediately adjoining the Wachong *finca*. I learned that during World War II, when Sam could not get there, Don Luis Wachong, as a friendly neighbor had taken over the management of Sam's farm for a period of months if not years. Now Sam was going down to his *finca* to make it more livable. Currently he and his wife were living in San Jose.

We spent our first night in Golfito. Here we stayed in a sparsely furnished hotel which Mrs. Wachong ran. She also ran the hardware store which was immediately next to the hotel. When it came time for dinner, we were taken out to a nearby Chinese restaurant.

At the end of the meal for our party of five or six, I started fumbling around to get some money to at least pay for my part of the meal. Sam saw what I was doing and came to my rescue saying, "Don't you know when Don Luis Wachong is around, you can't pay for anything?" I didn't, but I soon learned. I saw Luis Wachong Junior get up, go over to the manager, and come back to his father. I overheard him say to his father, "I signed the dinner bill and told him to take it out of next month's rent." So Don Luis Wachong owned this building too.

"Have you ever been to Da-vid (that is the way they pronounced it) in Panama?" I was asked by Don Luis the next morning. He wanted to take us to David, which is the first major city in Panama beyond the Costa Rica border. So we were off to Panama. We drove through the lush, green country side of Costa Rica. I had not even thought to bring my passport along . When we got to the border Don Luis got out and talked with Costa Rica border authorities and we got out of Costa Rica without me ever getting out of the car. With Don Luis Wachong, even crossing borders was no problem. It was very similar after we had driven the several hundred feet to the Panamanian entrance border immigration and custom officials. At David we saw several government buildings and a mosque. It was noon and we went to a Chinese restaurant with my genial host picking up the tab.

After viewing the local sights, it was back to Golfito. We reversed our procedures at immigrations and customs on the border, but no problems were encountered. I hesitate to think how long it would have taken me as a gringo without a passport and speaking no Spanish, to negotiate these two border crossings. I suspect it just would not have happened.

We got back to Golfito and had dinner at the canteen operated by the American Fruit Company. Don Luis asked if we wanted to see the banana ship being loaded, so after dinner we went down to the pier and we were invited to come aboard this huge freighter which was in the last stages of being loaded. Thousands of pounds of bananas had already been loaded.

The American Fruit plantation extended about ten miles inland where a small gauge railroad ran. The huge banana clusters with hundreds of bananas were cut from the trees, taken by hand to assembly points and hung on huge racks on the small railroad cars that were then pulled to the pier. Incidentally, I had learned in Golfito that Don Luis also owned the equipment for converting roasted coffee into powdered coffee.

The next morning we met up again and proceeded to the *finca*. We arrived at a clearing of several acres. The Wachong house was there, centered in a high barbed wire enclosure. We were served lunch soon after we arrived at the Wachong house. Inside the fence was a massive dog to discourage people from coming inside the compound.

Don Luis was anxious to see his cattle that were kept on the upper fields of his farm. So immediately following lunch, Don Luis invited me to see the cattle with him. The superintendent, Don Luis, his son, and I got saddled up. We already had spent two plus hours in the saddle in the morning, so with another two hours on a horse, I was tired and sore from being on any horse.

The biggest problem for me was the big tree stumps and fallen trees. Several huge trees had been cut down and left lying where they fell. We were sufficiently remote from civilization that it was too expensive to take them to a saw mill. The grass between the stumps grew four to five feet high. It was well up to the belly on the horse. Sometimes I could see the outlines of trees and sometimes I couldn't.

My strategy was to let the horse work it out for himself. This meant sometimes he tried to "crawl" over the bigger trees and sometimes he would go around the tree in an effort to keep up with others in the group. It was clear I was unable to keep up with Don Luis Wachong and the superintendent who wanted to find his prize bull. He had brought this animal in to improve the quality of his stock. At long last, when Don Luis and his superintendent had seen enough, we went back down the mountain to the Wachong house.

Earlier, I had found out I could go to a small airport about ten to twelve miles from the farm and fly back to San Jose. Don Luis had a truck going to the small airport for supplies. The driver could take me to that small airport. This we did the next morning. The driver spoke no English and I spoke little Spanish, but we made it. In the early afternoon I was deposited at a very primitive hotel in this very small town. I was now out from under the "protective arm" of my patron Don Luis Wachong. I was on my own.

It was Sunday, but it was a very special Sunday for it was Election Day. (Typically elections are held on Sundays in Costa Rica.) Here I am on Election Day in a foreign nation. What should a political scientist do, but go see how elections were conducted? I was undaunted by not knowing the local language. I felt I could find someone who would speak English and people there tried to be helpful.

So I walked around and saw several polling places and went to at least two. Voters were checked against a registration list, as one would expect. There were simple booths where printed ballots were marked in privacy. Everything was much as one would see at home, except the buildings were much simpler.

I went back to my most austere hotel room, having made arrangements for me to be awakened at 6:15 AM to make the 8:00 flight to San Jose. Everything seemed fine, but I was not prepared for the next event.

About 5:45 in the morning I was awakened by pounding on the door. A policeman was there. He spoke no English and I have already confessed that I spoke no Spanish and I did not have my passport. He made it clear that he wanted to see my identification. What could I show him? The only *picture* identification I had was my U.S. Army Reserve card which showed me to be a Colonel in the Intelligence Corps. This seemed to satisfy the policeman and I got to the airport and was flown back in a four person plane to the soccer field in the outskirts of San Jose.

Later I learned from Tom Gale, who was in San Jose as a semi-official contact for the University of Kansas, that he had been called by people from the American Embassy. They wanted to know "What was Drury doing down in Central Costa Rica on Election Day? What was a Colonel in the U.S. Intelligence service doing in there on Election Day? Had I tried to influence the election?" I had been the only foreigner there on Election Day. While Costa Rica is on friendly terms with the U.S., there was suspicion that the gringos from the north were trying to infringe on Costa Rican sovereignty. At that time an internationally notorious American, named Vesco, had gained residence status in Costa Rica and was resisting efforts of the U.S. to extradite him. Did Drury fit into the plot?

Poland

We had two experiences in Poland. Our first experience was in 1971. We stopped in Rome, on the way back from our son's wedding to Liesel Eiselen in South Africa. As it turned out, flight delays meant we spent an extra night in Rome and were able to visit briefly with the Ketzels who were in Rome at that time. We were headed to Poland where my colleague Jarek Piekalkiewicz and his wife Maura, were in Poznan, on a study grant. They had previously invited us to visit them in Poland, suggesting I might be able to learn something about local government there. Jarek had been in the Underground Resistance Movement in Poland during World War II and had somehow gotten to Ireland, where he met and married Moira. Both of these people are very outgoing and are some of our most cordial friends.

We took the train from Poznan back to Warsaw for our flight home. As we came out of the train station to look for a taxi to our hotel, we found a long line of people waiting for taxis. Fifty feet away there was a lone car. The driver approached us and offered us a ride. We asked him to take us to the Bristol Hotel. We soon became aware that he was driving faster and faster. I looked at Danny and asked under my breath, if she thought we should get out of the cab at the next stoplight. We decided not to, but when we got to the hotel, we discovered what was going on. The English speaking clerk at the desk asked us whether we had paid the driver, because the taxi inspector from the train station had been chasing us, as this man was violating the law by trying to make a few bucks on the side, as he was an unlicensed taxi driver. We said we had not paid him, and the offending taxi driver told the inspector that he was just a friend of ours, giving us a lift. We thoroughly expected that the "taxi driver" would return to see us to collect his fare. He never did and we were glad to not have been involved in anything more serious. During that frightening ride, Danny had feared for a few moments that perhaps we were being abducted or something equally sinister.

A decade after this first visit, Jarek was able to arrange for me and Cliff Ketzel to get a year lectureship at the University of Warsaw in an exchange program with KU. Cliff and I decided that Danny and I would take the fall semester and Cliff and Lee would take the second semester. It was 1980. I had always wondered about the meaning of the phrase "revolution was in the air." Living in Warsaw, we experienced the revolution in the air firsthand. There was a lot of political ferment and excitement which we could pick up on even though we didn't know Polish. During this time, Poland was still struggling for parliamentary democracy and total freedom from the communist system that had been imposed after the Second World War. This was finally achieved in 1989.

Traveling around Poland at Christmas time, I made sure I had plenty of U.S. dollar bills on my person, so that if we found ourselves in a troubled or dangerous situation, I could bribe someone to drive us over the border to safety. We were in Poland during "Solidarity" time – this was the movement for more freedom in Poland, and as more benefits came to the people, there were raises in salaries for university professors, so my salary went up four times in the three months we were there.

In general we found the Poles very friendly towards Americans. They liked to practice their English. I found, as I had in Japan, that my students were very interested in my English. Jarek's Aunt Sula was very friendly and cordial. For a foreigner, life in Warsaw was difficult. There were food shortages. Meat, sugar and butter were all rationed. We had a Polish friend who could buy meat that we were never able to buy even with our coupons, as local grocers saved certain cuts for their best customers.

One of my minor accomplishments was to arrange for Cliff and Lee to arrive in Warsaw to start their part of the exchange in the late afternoon and sit down to a dinner in their own apartment that evening, prepared by the maid we had hired. They liked the maid I had arranged for them so well that they hired her too.

While teaching in Poland, I can remember that I tried to familiarize myself with where I needed to go for a lecture the following day in a different location. I wanted to be on time for the lecture, so I got on the appropriate street car to go and find the venue. Without too much trouble I found the particular room where the lecture was to be held and was able to visit with the chairman of the department who was surprised to see me. It was a cold day and he offered me some brandy in his office. Later I arranged to invite him and a few other people to a small chamber music affair in one of the local castles.

PART 5:

Friends and Others

Mike March

In the years between 1936 and 1939, I came to know Mike as a fellow graduate student at the University of Illinois. Both of us had graduate scholarships at the university in the Political Science Department. These scholarships were awarded upon application to those whose grades qualified them, and in addition to the tuition, the scholarship paid us $300.

Mike was diligent in all his endeavors. Mike's mother and father were Russian. They had come to America and were working in the stockyards in Chicago when they met. They decided to move to a farm or homestead in Eastern Colorado. Mike told me that one of his jobs at home was to burn the thorns off of cacti using a blow torch, so that cattle could eat them.

As noted earlier, I looked Mike up when I was called to active duty in Washington D.C. in 1940. We lived together in Apartment 202. Most Saturday nights we went to dances for men in uniform at the Washington Hotel. One night Marion had come to the dance and a romance began between her and Mike that led to many years of happy marriage. Marion was one of the six or seven hundred young women that I and my fifteen or so recruiting officers had brought to Washington to work on codes and ciphers, so I like to think that in part I made their meeting possible.

Mike encouraged me to keep up with my United States Army Reserve (USAR) Program after the war ended. He knew the regulations and encouraged me to serve long enough to qualify for USAR retirement pay, which I did. I attended weekly meetings in Lawrence and annually went on active duty to Washington. I would spend my weekends between my two weeks of active duty each year with Mike and Marion who lived there. Typically Mike and I would do work around his yard when I was there. We would go to the hiring corner in Silver Springs on Saturday mornings and hire one of the men there to help us with yard work.

Mike and Marian had three children – Kathleen, Gregory, and Carolyn. Mike worked in the Bureau of the Budget of the Defense Department at the Pentagon. He was, at one time, accused of being a communist sympathizer. At this point he asked me to write a letter for him refuting such claims. This apparently helped, or at least it made it possible for him to continue to work on the Defense Department budgets.

After working at the Pentagon for a number of years, Mike and Marion decided to go to Harvard, where Mike received a Ph.D. in Economics. Typically one needs a language in a Ph.D. program, and Mike chose Russian due to his Russian heritage. Thereafter he took a job teaching at the University of Colorado.

Over the years Danny and I had many pleasant experiences with Mike's family. We went together on trips to Yucatan, Hawaii, and Alaska. Mike and Marion were gracious hosts in their home in Boulder, Colorado, where we occasionally would stop to visit them on our way to the Estes Park YMCA facility where we liked to vacation. Their house in Boulder had a perfectly handsome view of the surrounding areas. From their kitchen window one could see the mountains, and from the back of their home one could see downtown Boulder.

After Mike died we went to help Marion clear out some of his things. As we were clearing out one unit of bookshelves, I came across a little tobacco pouch behind some magazines on the top shelf. It was dirty and we almost threw it away but fortunately I opened it first and discovered three thousand dollars in cash! Marion did not know anything about it, but took the money to be deposited in the bank that very afternoon!

Danny and I consider it a real privilege to have had Mike and Marion as our life-long friends.

Professor Cliff Ketzel

I met Professor Cliff Ketzel while teaching at KU. He also taught Political Science. Cliff and I were both the only child in our families, but he was as close to a brother as I will ever have.

Danny and I did many things together with Cliff and his wife, Lee. When we went to Japan on our Fulbright, we rented our house to them. Later we exchanged visits in Lahore and Peshawar as we were both in Pakistan in the same year.

Cliff liked to do unusual things. He bought a VW Micro bus in Germany and drove it some of the way to Peshawar. Thoughtful of others, he would regularly pick up students walking to the university. I strongly suspect he was the one who maneuvered the Kansas Chapter of the American Society for Public Administration to honor me with an award. He was supportive of his sons' wives, encouraging them to get further education.

Cliff developed bowel cancer when he was around 50 and later he spent hours counseling other cancer patients. He was bubbly and enthusiastic, clearly evidencing that cancer patients can have pretty much a "normal life."

Cliff was one of the first people I knew, to realize that the Russians were *not* ten feet tall. He foresaw the collapse of the Soviet Empire in Western Europe and the disintegration of the Asian-Russian Empire. I remember how much he wanted to ride the train all the way across Russia.

We had many happy times together. After Cliff's untimely death, Danny and I have become even closer to Lee; we see her almost as a "sister-in-law."

Brushing Shoulders with U.S. Presidents

I had met President Herbert Hoover when I was in Princeton. Professor William Starr Meyers, one of my classroom professors, had just published his history of the Republican Party and the students had been alerted that Hoover would be at the regularly scheduled Sunday teas. This was enough to persuade us to go to shake his hand. I did go, and came away more aware that Hoover's timing had just been unfortunate for him. The Great Depression overwhelmed Hoover and most of the nation.

My second brush with a president came about in a very different way. Our little chapter of the American Society for Public Administration was struggling for members and meetings. The year I was President of the local chapter, I was encouraged by the Director of the Truman Presidential Library in Independence to bring our group to the library for an informal evening meeting with the former president. Harry Truman was willing to come down to the library after regular hours and give us a little lecture.

So I had the honor of introducing the former president to our group of forty or fifty who had chartered a bus from Lawrence and Topeka and were assembled in the comfortable little auditorium, which was part of the library. I remembered from my Speech 101 class, the more famous and well known the speaker, the shorter the introduction, so my introduction was very short. The President spoke for fifteen or so minutes and entertained a few questions.

PART 6:

Lawrence, Door County and Later Years

Door County

The Daniels Family (my in-laws) has long had an interest in Door County, Wisconsin. Danny's father suffered with hay fever from the ragweed pollens in Madison where they lived. With the assistance of friends, they found two lots on the sandy beach of Lake Michigan part way between

Danny and me in front of the Cabin

Jacksonport and Bailey's Harbor. On most afternoons, the breeze comes off the lake and has no pollens in it, which is great for hay fever sufferers. The Daniels found this property in the depths of the Great Depression in 1934. The owner of the lots was willing to sell, and at a price that was a small fraction of the worth of the lots today, as shore front beach property is in high demand.

When Danny's parents built their cabin on these two beach lots, there was no electricity. In 1948, when Wisconsin Public Service put in the power line, I started the wiring of the cabin and Mr. Erskine, an electrician, finished the job.

Danny and me on the beach at the cabin

Through a fortunate set of circumstances Danny's parents were able to acquire additional frontage due to the vacating of some land dedicated to roads to the beach. The roads had never been built. The Daniels gave the Drury's one hundred feet and in 1970 we had Ben Olsen, a local carpenter, build a small summer cottage, which we still call a cabin. The Drury family expanded when Jon, Jane, and Ann married and had children, and we then had a lumber company crew come in and build an addition, completed to "studs bare." I took over and completed the addition. We now have five bedrooms, two baths, a modest kitchen, a laundry room, a big living-dining room and a big storage area in the basement.

Danny has a special love of the cabin, which has been passed along to her children and their expanded family. Danny has come to her sandy beach here, for all but ten of the seventy-five years since 1934. The taxes may determine how long we can keep the cabin for us to use only sixty days a year.

View of the Cabin from the beach of Lake Michigan

An Unidentified Buyer
and Seven Uncertain Sellers

We were in Costa Rica three thousand miles away from Lawrence, when we first learned that an unidentified person wanted to buy our house on 15th Street in Lawrence. The house was only about seven years old, and we, having planned it and watched the construction, were in no mood to sell. Our good friend and long-time close neighbor, Eldon Fields, wrote that a real estate man, Guy Kidwell, had come uninvited to his door with a proposal.

The agent had a contract in his pocket all filled out except for the price. He wanted to buy Eldon and Cornelia's house. He could not say who the purchaser was or for what purpose the property was to be used. Eldon told him his house was not for sale and that he would do nothing in any event until he talked to his neighbors. He learned that the agent made similar calls to the adjacent property-owners.

Eldon suspected –and he was right – that we too would get such a visit when we returned from our trip to Costa Rica, two months later.

There were nine property owners in an area of about four acres immediately next to the University of Kansas. Our lot happened to be right in the center of this parcel of land. I felt that it was clear they could not do much with the other properties without ours. I told the real estate agent that, when he came to buy our property. I felt I had real leverage in any deal.

All of us were quite intrigued over this whole procedure. No one knew what was going on. We had different levels of attachment to our houses in this very attractive location next to the university. The owner of the vacant lot, Mrs. Underwood, sold to the real estate company. We were now down to eight reluctant potential sellers. In his visits with us, the agent had not mentioned any particular time frame. The unidentified purchaser was apparently willing to wait and "pick us off one at a time." This further raised our curiosity over this whole situation.

Was the purchaser going to build a filling station or some other equally undesirable building there? Would it be something which was compatible to the university? It was, at this point that we started to meet as a group to discuss what we could do. One meeting led to other meetings. Indeed, we had so many that Danny stopped attending. She did not want to sell. Period.

With a little encouragement, one of our group, Dr. Forrest Brown, our next door neighbor and a local dentist, became by general consensus, our chairman and our spokesperson. So he contacted the real estate agent only to find that he could get no additional information about the purchaser or why the purchaser wanted the ground. He did learn, however, that they were perfectly willing to deal with us as a group. We had to arrive at a price we would sell for and all of us had to agree to sell at the same time.

The ball was now in our court. What could we do with it? The obvious and critical question was price. Could eight families arrive at a figure that they were willing to accept and this unidentified purchaser would agree to?

I decided to investigate how much the typical land costs were of the total cost of a building. I assumed they would be building a structure that would cost $5,000,000. Frequently land values amounted to roughly 10% of the total. I then prepared a sheet to show how much each person's share of $500,000 would be. I used various formulas for dividing up the total sale price. One column showed each family's share if one used the current assessment of the property. Another showed the amounts if we used square feet of land involved. Maybe there were others, but it soon became evident that no one formula was clearly the best. Each of us saw the situation so differently.

In our group there was an employee from the Topeka DuPont plant that was expecting to be transferred and had no particular emotional attachment to his house. One of the KU professors was contemplating moving to another house in Lawrence. Another of our group had not built the house where she lived, but liked the location. She wanted to be able to see either the sunrises or the sunsets. Four of us had our houses built from plans we liked. Five of us taught at KU and the location meant a great deal to us—we could walk to work. What was a fair price for the acreage?

Finally it was decided that each of us would give Forrest Brown our price on a piece of paper, secretly without any group discussion. He would total them up, and give the figure to the real estate agent. This we did and the total was just over $500,000.

Somehow I learned that the owner of what I thought to be the nicest house was going to accept $90,000. I chose a price of $83,000, thoroughly expecting there would be a counter-offer and I would have to come down a bit. Frankly at $83,000 I had a little more than doubled the actual dollars I had in the house.

We gave the figures to Forrest on the weekend. Monday morning we got a call from Forest that they wanted us to come down about 2 %. There was no meeting on the subject, but Forest took the lead and told the buyer that we had so much difficulty arriving at the figure that he did not know how we could get together on another figure. So we would stand on our figure.

Within a short time, I got another call. The offer had been accepted. They would draw up the papers but we all had to sign at precisely the same time. It had to be a total package. We were to be in Forrest's living room at five o'clock on Friday afternoon to close the deal.

Five o'clock Friday came. We had heard "rumbles" that some people were not sure they had put in a high enough figure. They had agreed so easily to our figure we apparently were not asking enough. Would every one of our eight families "stay hitched?"

Everybody was there except our host, Forest Brown. One of his patients was having a problem and he had to stay in the office to take care of that sick patient.

The real estate agent decided that it would be all right if we would sign our contracts and let him hold them until he got all of them, including the one from Forrest. So each of us signed the legal deeds and went home. Shortly after we got back to our houses, Forrest got home, signed his contract, and then Guy Kidwell brought our contract to each of our houses. Thus we sold our house for $83,000. When I got the check, I realized it was the biggest check I had ever received.

The purchaser ended up being Phillips Petroleum of Bartlesville, Oklahoma. The management at Phillips were KU graduates and big supporters of the university and especially the football team. They built Jayhawk Towers, a huge multi-storied apartment complex with a parking lot. After several years, we understand they gave it to the university and the football team lives in some of the units. Almost certainly it became a tax write-off for Phillips Petroleum.

Though according to the contract we could buy back our houses and move them, no one did. The contract set a price for each of them, much higher than what they were eventually sold for to third parties. Each house was bought and moved.

1906 Marvonne Road

We moved to our house on Marvonne Road. We lived there until 2002. If one can love a house, I would say we loved 1906 Marvonne.

I was on the Lawrence Public Library Board from 1973-1977, when the "new" library building was built. I am proud to say that my name is on the plaque describing the library construction.

Under the rules in effect at the time, I retired from KU when I reached age 70, which occurred in 1989.

In 2002, after thirty seven years of living in the house on Marvonne Road, we moved to the retirement community of the Presbyterian Manor, with its several levels of care. We moved into an independent living unit. The duplex has a big living-dining area and adjoining kitchen, as well as a garage and two bedrooms and two bathrooms and we are very comfortable here.

My Children and Grandchildren

Jonathan Daniels Drury

In 1948 we had our first child, Jonathan Daniels Drury. When he started talking, we thought for several days that we might have a high powered mathematician on our hands. His first words were "one, two, three" - just as we had counted his drops of cod liver oil that we fed him every night at bath time - we had been advised that all babies needed the oil.

Jane, Danny, Ann and Jon

Danny and baby Jon

Jonathan went to Cordley and Hillcrest Elementary Schools, West Junior High, and to Lawrence High School. (Lawrence at that time had only one high school.) He went to KU for his Bachelor's Degree and then to the University of Illinois for his Ph.D. in Musicology. Romance developed between him and our AFS student, Liesel Eiselen. They were later married. After fourteen years there was a divorce, but only after two daughters, Danelle and Deline, were born.

Jon was married a second time, to Claire de Villiers, and from this marriage, Alyssa Joy was born. Claire died of breast cancer in 1996.

After living in Pretoria, South Africa for many years and teaching Musicology at the University of South Africa, Jon has retired and returned to Kansas. He has bought a five acre tract where he lives with his wife, Eleonora, and daughter Alyssa who is now in college in McPherson. Jon's eldest daughter, Danelle, studied musical theatre and education, and has recently moved from South Africa to the U.S. to pursue a performing career and is currently living with Jon and Eleonora in Kansas. Jon's middle daughter, Deline Drury Nourse, has married and is living in South Africa. She studied psychology and ministry/ theology. She and Crae, her husband, both work for rapidly growing Lonehill Methodist Church in Johannesburg, where they are two of its 25 full time staff members.

Claire and Alyssa Drury

Deline, Eleonora, Alyssa and Danelle

Me, Baby Danelle, Liesel and Danny at Danelle's Christening in South Africa

Deline, Jon and Crae Nourse

Liesel Drury née Eiselen

In 1970 we learned of the AFS program for the world wide exchange of high school students, and applied for a girl to pair up with Jane, our high school age daughter. After we were approved to have a student, AFS selected Liesel, from South Africa.

LIVING: AMERICAN STYLE — Liesel Eiselen, center, 18-year-old American Field Service exchange student from Pretoria, South Africa, joins in the harmonizing while her American "sister," Jane Drury, a Lawrence High senior, strums the guitar. Joining in the fun is Jane's sister, Ann, a seventh grader. Liesel arrived several weeks ago to live with the James Drury family, 1906 Maryonne Rd., and will attend LHS as a senior this year. Upon her return this June, Liesel, who speaks English and German as well as her native Afrikaan, will attend the University of Pretoria. (Journal-World Photo)

Ann, Liesel and Jane

We were in Door County for the summer so Liesel was sent to Milwaukee where we picked her up. She fitted nicely into our family, so nicely, in fact that our son Jonathan and Liesel got interested in each other. As a temporary solution we moved Jon out of our house once we returned to Lawrence. He moved into an apartment with two other KU students until spring when she returned to South Africa. The romance blossomed despite the distance. Jon sent her money and she bought an engagement ring in South Africa, since it didn't make sense to buy one in the U.S. when she was in South Africa where the diamonds come from. They arranged for a telephone call at Christmas time. As they talked, she put on the engagement ring. They planned for a June wedding in Pretoria, South Africa.

Danny and I went to South Africa for the wedding. In the first part of the service, a door of the sanctuary blew shut. The minister interrupted the proceedings to call out something in Afrikaans to the attendant at the door. We later learned that he had asked to have the door reopened as a South African custom required that the door be open so that anyone who desired to protest the marriage could enter and do so. The service was conducted in English and Afrikaans and the hymns were sung in both languages simultaneously.

Jon and Liesel remained married for fourteen years. They gave us two attractive and highly talented granddaughters - Danelle and Deline. Fortunately Liesel believes that children should know their grandparents and has kept in close touch with us. She writes long detailed letters of her comings and goings. We in turn have kept in touch with her and told her of major changes in our lives. Frankly her accounts are more interesting than ours. She has a real talent for writing.

Liesel is an exceptional and strong person and she drives herself with long and sometimes unusual hours. She has a small company for making videos - advertisements, corporate training videos and documentaries. She is most proficient in her work. We love her deeply and forget sometimes that she is not our own flesh and blood.

Deline, Danelle and Liesel

Jane Elizabeth Drury

Me, Jane and Danny on Jane's wedding day.
Jane wore the same dress Danny wore at our wedding 45 years earlier.

In 1952, our first daughter, Jane Elizabeth Drury was born in Lawrence. Jane attended Lawrence schools through high school and then went to Grinnell College in Iowa. While there she spent her junior year in Japan and still maintains an interest in all things Japanese and has been a member of the Japan–America Society for many years. After graduation, she tried the KU School of Business but found that it was not for her and turned to computers. She has had several computer jobs and in 2008, after working for 25 years at Sprint and then Embarq, she was offered too good a separation package to refuse. In 2009 she has begun working under short term contracts for various companies. She lives in Shawnee, a suburb of Kansas City, with her husband Russ Amos, who works out of his house as a highly skilled woodworker. They have two children - Lesli who is going to Boston University and Sean, who is still in high school.

Russ, Lesli, Jane and Sean

Ann Bernice Heyse nee Drury

In 1957, Ann Bernice Heyse (Drury) was born. She now lives in St. Louis and teaches English at a private high school. She has a Master's Degree in teaching reading. She has organized summer traveling and learning programs for her school and in 2008, she spent six weeks in Uganda as an exchange teacher. She and her husband David Heyse are active in their church. David works in a computer lab at Washington University. In 2009 their three sons have all "fledged" - Benjamin to MU at Columbia, Jonathan to Western Colorado University in Gunnison and Matthew to Colorado State College in Fort Collins.

Benjamin, Jonathan and Matthew Heyse

50th Wedding Anniversary, 1993

At one point we thought we might be able to arrange a big fiftieth wedding anniversary party, including the South African contingent of the family. We found, however that this was not possible because of Claire's health. Claire was my son Jonathan's second wife, and mother of his third daughter, Alyssa Joy. They were living in South Africa. She was suffering from breast cancer at the time of our fiftieth anniversary. Then it occurred to us that we might just do nothing special, but Ann especially, would have none of that, so we began to plan. And plan we did!

We decided we wanted something in our own house. This somewhat restricted us, but we decided that a sit-down dinner was our style. We decided we could fit a total of thirty two people in our downstairs room. H.G. and Kitty Morrison who had introduced us fifty years before, came from Washington, DC and Mike and Marion March whom we have known for all the fifty years we have been married came from Colorado.

We met the Marches and the Morrisons at the Kansas City airport on Friday afternoon, December 10. My youngest daughter Ann, and her husband, David Heyse and their three boys arrived from St. Louis in the early evening. As they drove up the driveway, our resident fox greeted them, posing in the headlights long enough for all five of the Heyses to see her and some of the kit foxes too. This was great fun for them.

Our house worked out well for our 450% increase in residents. The Morrisons were in beds in Jane's old room and Mike and Marion in Mother's study and Ann's room. The Heyses were downstairs in their suite.

On Saturday morning, I took some of our out-of-town guests to see the old Burdette Loomis House in Lawrence which is close to being an art museum, since they had filled it with many pieces of art. We then went to the river by the city hall and had the good fortune of seeing a Bald Eagle.

After lunch Ann presented us with a quilt with the hand prints of each of our children and grandchildren - including those from South Africa. These were in blocks with hand prints and signatures in different colored ink for each of our children's families. They ranged from Sean Amos, age four months, to Jon at 45. Ann had some glitches—like not receiving the panels of hand prints from South Africa in time to complete the quilt. She got the South African panels after one or more telephone calls, just before she planned to leave St. Louis to come to Lawrence and delayed their departure for two hours to sew the quilt together. She had to finish on Mother's sewing machine after she got here. She then had us put gold ink on our hands and print them on fabric blocks, which she added to the ones she had previously gotten and had sewn together. As it worked out there were exactly sixteen blocks, with each family's block being a different color. We displayed it on the fireplace in our Marvonne Road house for our guests to see when they arrived. Ann Thomas thought so highly of the project that she urged Ann to get into the business of making this kind of special hand printed banner or quilt. We later took Ann Thomas up on her offer to add some hand quilt-stitching to the quilt. The quilt now hangs in our hall way at the Presbyterian Manor, where it fits precisely, just as though it had been planned for that spot.

Our in-town guests and our daughter Jane and her family, from Kansas City, began to arrive at six. As chance would have it, December 11 in 1997 was on Saturday just as it had been fifty years earlier. Even the weather was much the same. We were really pretty ready for our other guests, thanks to so many helping hands.

As our guests began to settle in the living room the most common question was, "Tell us about that banner on the fireplace."

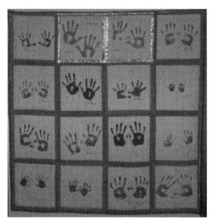

Our 50th anniversary quilt

After the gathering upstairs, we went downstairs for dinner. We had four tables with bright red table cloths, each seating 8 people. Our friend, Clarice Mulford, had insisted she wanted to provide the table decorations and this she did in the form of four identical beautiful floral centerpieces. I hesitate to think what it must have cost her. I asked her to use restraint — but I suspect she did not. The flowers were white snapdragons and some small white flowers. Each bouquet had greenery and three large lilies, which were white with red edges, and were quite dramatic, as Clarice had hoped they would be. We sent one home to St Louis with Ann and one to Kansas City with Jane as both were entertaining during the upcoming week. The room downstairs was lit with 50 tall white candles - some on the tables and others all around the room, so it looked very festive indeed.

On the north wall in the recreation room we had pictures of all the family. We also displayed Danny's wedding dress which Jane had used too, and the black lace gloves from Danny's great-great grandmother's 1845 wedding. (Those great-great-grandparentscelebrated their 67th wedding anniversary in 1912.)

After having wedding cake and ice cream for dessert, we went upstairs and sat around the living room. We had many stories told about us and our guests. I think everyone enjoyed it — I know Danny and I did. Our five grandchildren behaved beautifully. As soon as we finished, Ann and David got the boys to bed, albeit somewhat past their regular time. Jane and her husband, Russ, stayed for a while longer to help out. The family and our guests had all the dishes done before we went to bed.

On Sunday, the eleven people in our house had a leisurely breakfast. H.G., Mike and I took the Heyse boys to the playground to work off some of their excess energy. The Morrisons wanted to take all of us out to dinner. We arranged for Jane and family to join us at a fancy brunch in Kansas City, which was just off the highway that Ann and David had to take to get to St. Louis. So they were a little way on their return trip to St. Louis and well fortified with food.

A very festive occasion indeed!

The couple around their golden wedding anniversary

The Drury Reunion: 2000, Door County - Two, six, ten, thirteen, eleven, eleven, six, and two

Such were the numbers of people at our family reunion at 6890 Highway 57 in Door County, Wisconsin. It all began on Sunday morning, June 24 at 7:30 when Danny and I left our cabin to make the five hour drive to Chicago, to meet the South African contingent of our family (minus our son Jon) at O'Hare International Airport.

Their flight was due to arrive at 4:45PM, but just to be on the safe side, we arrived at O'Hare at about 2 PM with books to read while we waited for them to come. We got to the terminal and their flight number was not on the screen so we asked an attendant about the Sabena flight from Brussels and she said a Sabena flight from there was just arriving. We watched some people come out and then tried again to get information on their precise numbered Sabena flight. Danny decided to keep watching and lo and behold, there were Liesel, our former daughter-in-law, and our three South African granddaughters.

We had our hugs and kisses and found that all three had been moved up to the earlier flight because the travel agent had booked Alyssa, our youngest granddaughter, on a separate flight and the airlines would not let her go by herself, nor let one of the older children use her ticket. So the airlines found space for all four on the earlier flight, but that meant they would be separated from their luggage.

After an hour of wrestling with the airlines on the luggage problem, we were off in our car to our downtown hotel. Our party of six got checked in and after a minimum of refreshing, went out for a walk across Michigan Avenue to Buckingham Fountain and to a very nice park right on the lake with a marina full of boats.

Back at the hotel, we found the Chinese restaurant in the hotel open and in due course went there for our evening meal. We were about the only ones in the restaurant. We all went to our rooms and the South Africans had to get by with only their carry-on luggage.

Some of us had a "pick-up" breakfast the next morning. We had heard from Jane, our daughter and her husband, Russ who had arrived in the Chicago area on Saturday and were staying Saturday night and Sunday night with a college friend in the outskirts of Chicago.

As planned Russ, Jane, and their children, Lesli, and Sean appeared at about 10:15 AM. Fortunately they were able to get into their room and unloaded their luggage. All ten of us piled into Russ and Jane's van and we set off for a little ride to the more affluent areas a bit north on Michigan Avenue. We saw the Navy Pier, and Russ got parked in public parking near the art gallery. This was to be our first stop for the day.

Our group split according to interests but agreed to assemble for lunch in the museum cafeteria at 12:30. There was more of the same after lunch. I chose to go mostly to the Impressionist section, but also enjoyed the collection of miniatures depicting individual rooms in houses, castles, and the like, over a long span of history. These miniatures were all done to scale and showed how people lived at various times. Some of the group chose to go back to the hotel with Russ, but Jane and I walked the three-quarters of a mile back to the hotel.

At 6:00 PM we assembled and walked the several blocks on Michigan Avenue to Bennigan's (a national chain restaurant) —a place a little more pretentious than the not-so-inviting Chinese restaurant at the hotel. I can still remember Liesel ordering, and obviously enjoying, a big T-bone steak. Nobody wanted to go back to the Chinese restaurant in the hotel.

After a leisurely supper we set out on foot for about a mile walk to see the lights of Chicago from the top of the Sears Tower, one of the tallest buildings in the world. It was quite spectacular. It was a clear evening with a great view in every direction. We walked back to our hotel — Liesel found her shoes uncomfortable and chose to go barefoot on the sidewalks of Chicago to get back to the hotel. We were hoping that the luggage would be at the Hotel, but alas, it was not.

Tuesday morning I had some of my special present of rusks (a special South African kind of sweetened toasted bread). Most had breakfast in the snack bar of the hotel and then we went off on foot to the Aquarium for the third of our special attractions in Chicago. We timed things right to get to the dolphin show which featured the dolphins walking on their tails across the water.

From there we went across the street to the Field Museum. Everyone saw Sue — the best preserved Tyrannosaurus Rex. We had lunch and then split up according to our interests. Can you imagine trying to keep six adults and four children together in this huge museum?

About 3:30 PM Danny and I gave out – sight seeing is hard work! We wanted to get back to our hotel. The walk back to the hotel seemed a little far. We waited in line for the free bus, but it never came. We gave up and took a city bus back to the hotel. Three of the four suitcases were there, but not Liesel's.

Walking back the previous night, Russ Amos had seen a sign about Chicago Style Pizza and suggested that for supper. We called a place about five blocks from the hotel and got there to find it was in the basement and very noisy. At the adjoining table was a group of ten to twelve people who were having a training session for waiters. The trainer had a loud, loud voice and was trying to keep the attention of the group to keep them involved. I could hardly hear myself think. I was at the end of the table and could not really take part in the discussion at the other end of our table — and a hearing aid would not have helped.

Wednesday was the day of our departure from Chicago. Russ and Jane had, on the previous Sunday, gone to the Science and Industry Museum and so they set off for the Planetarium and then to their friends' house where they had left bicycles which they wanted to get to the cabin. Then they drove on to Madison. Plans had been made to go to Madison to allow the South Africans a chance to see Farrington and Alice, Danny's brother and sister-in-law.

So six of us loaded up three bags from South Africa - Liesel's bag was still missing. She had had to spend hours on the phone. There had been a worldwide search for her bag without any results. And we were off for the Science and Industry Museum - about three miles south of our hotel. We chose various parts of the huge Museum to visit, had lunch, then more looking, and at 2:00 PM we set out for Madison, Wisconsin. We had reservations at a motel which we knew to be near a Bonanza Steak House. Everyone had liked the place the previous year when we had met the Heyse boys as they were coming back from their summer camp, and Ann, our other daughter, her husband David, and his mother, Marie, as they were coming back from Ireland.

We got checked into the motel and invited Danny's nephew, Chris Daniels and his family of five to join our ten for dinner at Bonanza. After supper we all went to visit Danny's brother and sister- in-law, Farrington and Alice. Chris felt they could stand all fifteen of us descending on them at once and so we did.

The living room at Alice and Farrington's house on Piper Street was wall to wall with people, visiting, reminiscing, and of course taking many pictures. With six of our fifteen under ten, we felt we had to make the visit shorter than Farrington wanted, but we did promise to return on the morrow.

Madison Gathering: Back row: Cheryl, Russ Amos, Owen, Lesli, Deline, Danny, Chris and Alice Front row: Me, Sean, Alaina, Farrington, Alyssa, Liesel, Marianna, Danelle

By now it was Thursday morning and Liesel had no luggage so we found a discount store that opened at eight in the morning. After the continental breakfast provided by the motel, we left Mother doing laundry at the motel and set out shopping to get Liesel some clothes. We were about their only customers and the South Africans had a "field day" comparing prices in the U.S. and South Africa. Bare essentials were purchased with a few extras that could hardly be described as essentials, such as the book *Chicken Soup for the Soul* for people of Alyssa's age (10) — I did not know there were such books.

We wanted to see Chris and Cheryl's hundred year old house. We were all impressed with its size and spaciousness, very different from the houses being built today.

Then we went to the Farrington Daniels Chemistry Building. Unfortunately they were doing some construction and the name plate on the building was obstructed by a fence which some of the group managed to move away so that we could all have our pictures taken in front of the cornerstone of the building with Dad Daniels's name on it. We went into the office and asked to see the bust of Farrington that had been made by his wife, Olive. Due to construction, they weren't sure where it was, but they found it in the office of the Chairman who happened not to be around. However, the office secretary was pleasant and presented us with a thick book on the history of the department. In the index were many references to Farrington Daniels.

Danny, Deline, Alyssa, Sean, Lesli and Danelle at the
building named for their great grandfather – Danny's father.

Next we went to see 1129 Waban Hill - the house that Olive and Farrington, Danny's parents, had built in 1921. We introduced ourselves to the "lady of house" who almost certainly was a maid or baby sitter. We were not invited in, but did walk up the driveway a bit and encountered a carpenter-remodeler who was building a deck on the back. He volunteered that he had taken out the closets which the previous owner had added to the house.

Our second visit at Farrington and Alice's house was our next stop. There was more visiting and telling of stories and at about 12:30 we headed for 6890 Highway 57, our cabin. (We call it a cabin, but most "cabins" don't have two bathrooms, a modern kitchen, and beds for twelve.) We had decided not to try to stay together in our driving but Lesli and Alyssa, cousins born just 5 days apart, were getting along so well together that Alyssa joined Lesli in the Amos family car.

We arrived about 4:45 and the Amos contingent came a little later. Ann and David and Matthew, their youngest, had prepared a nice dinner for us and for the first time in many years, Ann was able to get reacquainted with Liesel and to meet her two grown-up nieces again.

Then at 10:30 PM a phone call came. Liesel's luggage had been found! It was in the hands of a woman at the Green Bay Airport whose job it was to deliver it. We described our driveway at 6890 Highway 57. We hung shirts on the road to help her find it, and about midnight, Liesel finally got her bag. So on Thursday night, after her having checked the bag at Johannesburg International on the previous Saturday night, she at last had her clothes.

The first two nights, Mother and I got dinner. Life became more leisurely - no museums, skylines, or traffic to fight. There was just eating, sleeping, swimming and game playing. We had unbelievably nice weather. We had one day with high waves and with the assistance of the middle generation I got in and had a wonderful time jumping the waves.

Sunday was the Door County Dairy breakfast and we all went there and had our fill of pancakes, scrambled eggs with ham and the trimmings, and also ice cream bars. That evening we declared our birthday dinner for just about everyone, and Mother and I put on our typical turkey dinner — come to think of it we missed having the candied sweet potatoes.

On Monday the Amos family treated all of us to a "fish boil" at the Square Rigger. I think it was a first for the South African girls (except Alyssa.) I think many - at least some of us - me included, ate too much. We came back to Russ Amos's extensive fireworks display on our beach.

Tuesday was the official Fourth of July and we planned ahead and got one of our cars parked at a good viewing spot for the Bailey's Harbor parade. We then went back later to claim our spot. Our spot was close to the beginning of the parade and the kids got huge quantities of candy, thrown by the people on the floats. At noon, Mother wanted a typical Fourth of July picnic on the beach — brats from Viola's store and the contest as to who could spit the watermelon seeds the farthest. After supper it was off again to Bailey's Harbor for their "professional" fireworks. They started a little late but they were fun.

Wednesday was departure day for David and Matthew Heyse (Ann's youngest.) They were going camping, then attending family night at Benjamin's and Jonathan's camp (Ann's other two boys) and then bringing the boys back to the Cabin. So we were down to eleven at our cabin with Ann moving back to our cabin from D6 – the cabin next door, so named for the six Daniels that had summered there in Danny's youth.

Thursday, another couple called David and Ann (Ludwig) arrived at D6 from their home in Orlando, Florida. It is a strange coincidence that our daughter Ann was born on the same day as her cousin David Ludwig years ago. And our daughter Ann married David Heyse and David Ludwig married Ann Rutledge.

David and Ann Ludwig had Michael, 9 years old, and Claire, 3 years old, with them. The Ludwigs try to get to the cabin every several years and this worked out especially nicely this year with so many cousins around.

Friday saw David Heyse and his three sons arrive shortly after Russ and Jane and family left for Kansas. We were down to eleven in our cabin — but now a slightly different eleven. We decided it was laundry day and we had huge quantities for the LeClair Laundromat (We don't know the story, but find in 2009, the building is completely gone.)

On Saturday Chris and Cheryl arrived at D6 and before long, arranged for a fancy dinner party on Sunday at an upscale place in Door County for the middle generation — The Daniels, the Heyses, the Ludwigs, and Liesel.

We thought Grandpa and Grandma were charged with taking care of the small fry Sunday night. We were not aware that plans had been afoot for the small fry to do things at D6 with Danelle and Deline, our oldest granddaughters, babysitting so that Mother and I could rest in the quiet of our cabin. Instead we kept everyone over at our cabin to the children's consternation. We learned of the planned arrangements only after the middle generation got back and then the small fry went over for more celebrating at D6. We hope their future was not irrevocably spoiled.

Monday saw Chris, Cheryl, and family returning to Madison. The Heyses left Tuesday morning and we were down to six at the Cabin.

Many things are not included in this summary. There were many trips in which only some of the group participated. A group walked to Jacksonport. There was an excursion to Peninsula State Park as well as a trip to Al Johnson's restaurant. I had prepared a list of some twenty things to do in Door County. Liesel pointed out on the next to last day that they had done all but two.

Wednesday morning at 7:40, the South Africans and Mother and I left in a loaded car for a 1:00 PM arrival at O'Hare for a four o'clock departure. Liesel needed an extra hour to get a mislaid ticket replaced – Alyssa's ticket was missing! I felt we had to leave time for traffic snarls and a possible flat tire in the 250 mile trip.

We planned a luncheon stop at the Oasis restaurant which straddles the Chicago toll way. This was the very place where Liesel had made a telephone call about her luggage ten plus days before. After searching the cabin for the missing plane ticket, we decided we would at least ask at this place to see if there was a "lost and found" that might have the ticket. After two referrals we got to the manager of Wendy's, Lori. She disappeared and within a minute was back with an envelope with "Miss Alyssa Drury" written on it containing her ticket. How about that? Thousands of people pass through there every day. Lori hardly stayed long enough for us to thank her.

We continued on to O'Hare. We had no problem getting to the departure terminal. Having said our goodbyes at the last stop, Danny went in to check that the flight was on time. I stayed with the car and had no trouble with the police wanting me to move, so I just waited. In about twenty minutes all five appeared and I got out of the car and started a second round of hugs only to see two tow trucks coming rapidly, ready to remove all parked cars. I rushed back to our car. The tow truck driver waved understandingly and in a friendly way. We got into the car and drove away, waving to our departing South African family.

Five hours later we were back at the cabin in time for supper. We were back to our starting number — two. Approximately 24 hours later Liesel telephoned that they were home with their entire luggage.

Such a grand and glorious time all of us did have!

Our 60th Wedding Anniversary

Danny's sister, Mino and her brother, Dorin both came from Oregon for this occasion. We held the dinner in the recreation room of the Manor. We had it catered by HyVee, and ran out of coffee during the party, and they had to brew and bring more. We rented dishes and tablecloths and spent a lot of money on flowers. We had about forty eight people. Our daughter Ann sprinkled the tables with little silver confetti-like decorations.

Cutting the cake on our 60th wedding anniversary

Our 65th Wedding Anniversary

The family at our sixty-fifth wedding anniversary celebration

It happened that the wedding date in 1943 had much the same kind of weather as the day of our 65th wedding anniversary – cold and gloomy. Our 65th anniversary was celebrated in Lawrence, Kansas. We had a sit-down dinner at Alvamar Country Club with approximately fifty people in attendance – we consider this our contribution to the federal government's Stimulus to the Economy Program! Of course included were my bridge foursome and their partners and people whom we have known for years and years. Six of our eight grandchildren were there – only the two South African granddaughters that were living in South Africa, were absent.

A family member hosted each table and Earl Nehring stepped in for the remaining table when we ran out of family members.

Danny and Me on our 65th anniversary

PART 7:

Travels

Throughout our lives we have been on many trips both within the U.S. and abroad. We have visited Yucatan, Mexico, England, China, Japan, Hong Kong and South Africa among others.

Me in front of Long Lake, Colorado

Many of our trips both abroad and in the U.S. were Elderhostel tours. We liked Elderhostels so much that we attended about 25 over the years. Nowadays the price of Elderhostels has gone up significantly and they are not the exceptional deal they used to be. Most of the people that go on Elderhostels are educators like us and people with a sense of adventure.

The programs usually included three subjects – the local history of the area, the natural surroundings and view sites, as well as visits to museums or galleries of interest. Many times, special interests, such as birding, were emphasized, and this drew many people.

Below I expand on a few of the most memorable trips.

Prince Edward Island, Canada

When we visited Prince Edward Island, we had to access it by ferry from mainland Canada. When we were there they were beginning the construction of a splendid new bridge from the island to the mainland, which has since provided easier movement to and fro, and the forecast was that this would be a big stimulus to the economy of the island. There was however some opposition to the bridge being built, as people were unhappy about the changes that the bridge would bring to the island.

When they were driven out of Canada by the English, a number of the French immigrants, the Acadians, went to New Orleans, where they have become the Cajuns and an important part of that community. Some of the Acadian French, have however remained on Prince Edward Island and are anxious to preserve their French ancestry and culture, including their French language, so it was interesting to learn about some of the problems of this minority group.

The story of Anne of Green Gables, which has become a much loved story around the world, is set on the Island, and we were able to visit Green Gables – the home of Lucy Maud Montgomery, the author.

On our visit, a friendly lobster man showed us how, by using modern global positioning satellite technology to locate his submerged lobster cages, he no longer had to remember where his lobster cages had been placed.

I found it unusual that people on Prince Edward Island had founded many co-operatives. They had found that the co-operative system, and cutting out the middle man, saved them a lot of money, in, for example, transporting their fishing harvests to New England. They then went on to develop many co-operatives-- even one for burials.

Corning, New York

The Stueben Glass-works factory and museum on the history of glass making were very interesting and well worth a visit. Man has been doing wonderful and beautiful things with glass. These glass ornaments are so highly prized that they have frequently been given to chiefs of state by our American presidents, as gifts. Our untutored eyes could not tell the difference between "perfect firsts" – the highest quality of glass ornaments made there, and "imperfect seconds." We bought a slightly imperfect "seconds" little bear. The Elderhostel program also included a visit to the Museum of Western American Art as well as a stop at a museum depicting life in the area in the 1790s.

Monticello, Virginia

As admirers of Thomas Jefferson, we had tried several times to get in to the limited Elderhostel quota for the tour of Monticello, the estate of Thomas Jefferson, where he lived with several hundred slaves. The tour's emphasis was on the gardens and Jefferson as a horticulturist. He experimented with and grew various kinds of plants and cross pollinated plants to create his own varieties. He had his own smithy, in which tools that he needed, could be created. Monticello was largely a "free standing" community. It grew its own food and preserved it for the non-growing season.

I had hoped there might be more focus on Jefferson as a politician. However we learned interesting things. After Jefferson's presidency, people would often come and call on him unannounced, and common courtesy called for them to be fed and put up in some style. He found this became a fiscal drain on him and he had all kinds of problems with his finances. I think at one point he came close to declaring bankruptcy.

Some of the employees at Monticello affectionately referred to Jefferson as "TJ." Perhaps in this way he seemed closer to them, rather than a two century old hero. I learned that TJ was not good at giving speeches. It seems it is now a generally accepted fact that he had an affair with Sally Hemmings and that he sired some mulatto children.

Birding trip to Corpus Christi Texas and Galveston

We took two Elderhostels to this area – both were birding trips. As you may know, birds love to go to garbage dumps. At Corpus Christi, we found all kinds of birds swarming around the spots where the garbage trucks were. This was the place where Mary

Allen, our long time friend, established her reputation among the whole bus load of people, as a competent birder. I have joked with her that she should pay me a finder's fee for her getting the job of being a bird expert for a later Elderhostel session. But of course, I never got my finder's fee. At Galveston, in addition to bird study, we had talks on the local history of the area. A fifth of the population of Galveston was killed by a hurricane in 1900.

Marble Canyon

We went on an Elderhostel to Marble Canyon at the east end of the Grand Canyon. One of our speakers on that trip was a professional cow-girl. While there we visited the Power Plant of the massive Hoover Dam. Thousands of tons of concrete have been poured into the Colorado River channel to block the water from taking its natural course and enable the region to have low cost electric power.

Grand Canyon West

We took another Elderhostel trip to Grand Canyon West, where a tribe of Indians is desperately trying to develop this area as a special sightseeing paradise. On the south rim, you look north several thousand feet to a cave in which literally tons of very valuable bird droppings have accumulated for centuries. Now they are mining this as fertilizer. There is a beautiful viewpoint, looking back east into the canyon. After paying a small fee to the Indian tribe involved, we were able to drive down to the river itself and to put our feet in the water. This is also a take-out point for the boats that go through the canyon.

Grand Canyon

We ought to have a more superlative word to describe the biggest and most beautiful of all canyons in the world. When visiting the

Canyon, one can stay either at the south rim or at the north rim. I have stayed at both but I much prefer the north rim. While I lack precise figures, I estimate there are perhaps a thousand times as many visitors to the south rim as to the north rim. One has to drive about one hundred and fifty extra miles on good highway to get to the north rim, but in my mind it is well worth it as there are so many fewer crowds. At the north rim we have stayed in rather flimsy wooden two-family units, but we find the view of the canyon better from this side.

The park at the south rim has limited roads to view sites and these are crowded with tour busses and cars. When I was last there I almost needed a number to be able to get a view of the canyon.

Alaska

Danny and me in Alaska

We went to Alaska on two separate occasions; once on an Elderhostel tour and once on a cruise.

The cruise to Alaska was a most interesting experience for us. We were able to buy tickets on a small cruise line, operating approximately 90 passenger ships. Such ships are able to get much, much closer to the calving glaciers than bigger ships, as thousands of tons of ice cascade into the ocean. On the Majestic Explorer we could go very close to the calving glaciers that would drop off into the water with tremendous noise and splashing. We could look at the mountainside in Glacier Bay and see where the glaciers had receded and how the land was being formed. It was as if we could see the earth being created. Probably a mile from where the calving was taking place, there was solid rock, and then in another mile there would be a little green of some vegetation. Another mile and there would be larger plants. This continued until we saw trees growing.

We were told a fascinating story about what had taken place on the ship (Majestic Explorer) we were on at a previous time. A woman suffering from terminal cancer had always wanted to cruise to Alaska. The then-Captain of the ship got the small ship hung on a rock, due to misjudging the tides. It was decided that all passengers should get into life boats, for fear that the ship might tip off the rock as the tide lowered. Passengers were told to move away so that the crew could lower the life boats. All passengers were to be evacuated from the ship while the crew got the ship back in the water. The cancer-ridden woman did not move out of the way and was killed by a life boat being lowered. The Captain was relieved from his command and the Chief Engineer was given command of the ship. The ship had to go to port and dry dock to be examined to determine its seaworthiness after this close call.

The Elderhostel was to Mount Denali National Park, to one of the highest peaks in Alaska. We saw bears and many beautiful flowers. After the Elderhostel we drove ourselves to Anchorage, Fairbanks and Prince Rupert Sound to see more of the wonderful Alaskan scenery.

Bellingham, Washington

H.G. and Kitty Morrison arranged for us to attend this National Wildlife Federation Convention in Bellingham, Washington. It was a very well organized event with about three thousand people attending. We went on a bus trip to the mountains and hiked across a nearby island.

We attended various lectures and interest group talks. We stayed in a beautiful place right on the coast. We took this opportunity to visit Dorothy Arnold, a roommate of Danny's when they lived in Washington, D.C. Dorothy and her husband lived in a very beautiful area and took their small ocean-going ship on little trips. Unfortunately, four years after our visit, Dorothy died of cancer.

International Falls, Minnesota

International Falls, Minnesota, borders on Canada and is normally the coldest spot in the continental United States. We took this Elderhostel trip to allow our daughter Ann to celebrate her fortieth birthday, with some friends, in the cabin, where we usually summer. I remember finding, twenty miles off of the main route, a road that paralleled the border into Canada. There we found a State Park where there was a trained guide to explain the park's unusual natural environment. We learned about Indian burial mounds that are more than a thousand years old, of which there are many in this area. We also visited the Voyageurs National Park and a local paper mill. We took trips in canoes, similar to those that the French fur traders used to travel further south to Lake Superior in bygone days.

Spain

We took an almost three week Elderhostel trip to Spain. We went from Madrid, north to Pamplona and saw the second running of the bulls. The first running of the bulls is the bigger, more famous event, and is described by Hemmingway in one of his novels. This happens earlier in the year. After we saw the second running, we then joined the parade and marched through the streets with the locals, once the bulls had passed. Some people run ahead of the bulls and try to keep from getting gored.

We learned a lot about the fifteenth century pilgrim route -- the Way of St. James--from France to Northwestern Spain. Over two centuries, hundreds of thousands of pilgrims walked from France, over the Pyrenees, and along Northern Spain to a famous cathedral, Santiago de Compostela, on the sea where the remains of Saint James are supposed to be buried. Inns, burial grounds, eating places --all were developed along this route, to take care of all the pilgrims.

For years I had wanted to see the Alhambra in Southern Spain. I had first learned about it from the writings of Washington Irving. Our young guide did not think much of Alhambra, so he gave us very little time to see it. It is a magnificent Moorish Palace with classic lines of architecture.

South Africa

Over the years I made about four trips to South Africa. Danny made many more, as she was freer to travel and wanted to see our grandchildren grow up. One of the most memorable trips must be the trip along the Garden Route and to Cape Point, where one can look out over the Indian Ocean on the one side and the Atlantic Ocean on the other side of the point. We drove from Cape Town to East London, where we met Jon, our son, and Claire, his wife. We drove through the Transkei and stayed in a former tuberculosis rehabilitation center that had been made into a bed and breakfast by the Transkei government. The hostess was the daughter of the Transkei Education Minister and was most entertaining in her own right. From the vantage point of the bed and breakfast on the high hill overlooking the sea, we were able to see many ocean vessels passing by the site.

Another memorable trip was to the Pilansberg Game Reserve with Jon and Claire, Deline and Danelle. We stayed in tent-like accommodations and the toilets and showers were in an enclosure nearby and were open to the skies. There was only cold water to shower under. My granddaughters remember with much amusement, how I called for a chair to put over the shower cubicle when it started to rain while I was showering.

We would leave the campsite daily to go on game drives. On one such occasion, the monkeys figured out how to unzip our tent, and they stole much of our food supply. I was not so keen to go out after that and spent many hours guarding our supplies while sitting on the porch of the tent, throwing half eaten fruits at the thieves in the trees, much to the family's amusement.

Rome Seminar with Jim Seaver and a Sad Unexpected Trip to South Africa

Jim Seaver presented a KU seminar summer program in Rome and Danny and I went along for the ride as auditing students – we sat in on the classes and learned much about Rome, but did not have to take the tests. Jim Seaver is very knowledgeable about history and talked of the various Roman emperors, as if they were close friends of his. Jim Seaver had advised that we keep our billfolds in our front pockets and secure them with safety pins. I had done so, but one day the seminar group was travelling by bus on our way to visit some of the ruins. As we got off the crowded bus on which I had been standing, I realized my billfold was missing. I yelled to the bus driver to explain the problem, but no one could help. Fortunately I had left most of my valuables at the hotel, but the money I had packed for the day and my driver's license was gone.

On this trip to Rome, we saw the town of Pompeii, as well as many of the famous buildings, architectural spots and famous Roman ruins. Towards the end of our stay in Rome, my daughter, Jane reached us by telephone at supper one evening with bad news. She told us about Claire's (our daughter- in-law in South Africa) serious condition with cancer, which had just returned with a vengeance after being in remission for a while. We decided that we should go to South Africa. We couldn't get a flight until the next day.

Jon and Claire had an unlisted telephone number and so we had to call Liesel, our former daughter-in- law, from Rome, to get the number to let Jon know when we would arrive in South Africa. Jon was able to meet us at the airport and we went directly to Claire's room in the hospital. The room was full of flowers and Claire had many visitors. Claire was very lucid, and at one point there were a strange assortment of visitors in her room – Jon's ex-wife, Liesel and their two daughters, Claire's brother's ex wife and her daughter, as well as Claire's brother and his current girl friend. The nurse said that only family could stay in the room, and Claire responded, "But we are all family!"

We stayed in South Africa for two very stressful weeks and then left with Jon's permission. Claire passed away about 24 hours after our departure.

Sumitomo Bank, 1996

In 1955 when we left Japan after our Fulbright year in Sendai, we had extra yen left over. The Fulbright program had been generous to us. We had lived in Sendai where things did not cost as much as in Tokyo. So we bought all the things we thought we could use, but wound up with extra yen equivalent to $350. I invested this yen with two companies but later consolidated it with Sumitomo Bank - one of the very big banks in Japan.

Over the next forty years we had correspondence about the money and it seemed to grow. Of course, one of the features was that with 360 yen to a U.S. dollar in those days we would get these statements about the big numbers of yen and think of them as dollars, but then we knew that was not right. Every two or three years, I would write and someone different would respond.

To make a long story short, when we got reports of our holdings in Yen, we would tell them to reinvest the money and some-day we would come to claim it. There was always an element of uncertainty about it, for we knew we wanted to get back to Japan, but were not at all sure we ever really would. The numbers of yen seemed so large we almost thought of the yen as a kind of play money. We were uncertain as to whether they would actually give us the money to spend, if we ever got to Japan. When our daughter, Jane, was in Japan, spending her college junior year abroad, she was able to use some of the money.

In August 1996, when it was clear that we were in fact going to go to Tokyo, I wrote to try to get instructions on how I would get this money. I wrote to the man from whom I had last gotten a letter. We did not hear... and did not hear... so I arranged to get someone who spoke Japanese to go with me to my Lawrence bank. I sent a second letter and shortly I got a telephone call apologizing for not answering earlier, but telling me to see him, Mr. Suzuki at his bank, upon my arrival in Japan, and I could get the money and be off for Sendai in 15 minutes.

The $350 of 1955 had become $8,034.87. Would we ever really get it? I was sufficiently uncertain that I had purchased travelers' checks in dollars for us to use in Japan and three weeks in Hong Kong, if there were a hitch and we did not get the money.

The fateful day arrived. We had a commitment to meet friends in Sendai in a few hours. We would have to go to the huge central Tokyo railroad station and find the right train to Sendai, so time was an important consideration. We had a room in the downtown hotel and our interpreter came to meet us there. We got instructions on how to get to the Sumitomo bank building, which as it turned out, was only a short walk from our hotel.

It was 9:55 AM when the three of us (Danny, the interpreter and I) went up to the door of this big, impressive, many-storied bank building. It looked like it was an automatic door but it did not open when we approached even though we could see many people in the bank. We noted the hours were posted and the bank was supposed to open at 10:00 AM. We stepped back and waited. At precisely ten o'clock we went up to the door and then it opened. We entered and saw about thirty clerks all standing stiffly at their desks and facing us. As we walked in, they looked toward us and bowed in unison, saying, "Ohio Gozaimus" (Good Morning.) My! What an unexpected greeting for someone with a small account. We thought that maybe this was their way of greeting customers who have had accounts for more than forty years. We walked across the big lobby to a receptionist and asked to see Mr. Suzuki, but as we came up to the receptionist, we saw a young man coming up from the back row of desks. It turned out that it was Mr. Suzuki and he was there to help us.

Later we learned that the warm welcome we got was something that they did every day for their first customer of the day.

Mr. Suzuki prepared papers and soon he had our money - over $8000 in Japanese yen. Their biggest bill is 1000 yen. With the exchange rate of 300 yen to one U.S. Dollar, we had a huge pile of thousand yen bills. Mr. Suzuki took them over to a special counting machine to verify that there were the correct number of bills. The pile was so thick that one could not fold them. Should we take them and leave? Yes, he said, this was a lot of money. He suggested taking half of it in travelers' checks and half in cash. When I agreed, he went away but then came back quickly and said their travelers' check department did not open until 10:30. Did we still want travelers' checks? As we were discussing this, another official came up and said they could make an exception and issue them now, but it would take a few minutes. Getting the money turned out to take three quarters of an hour rather than the 15 minutes we had budgeted, but we made our train to Sendai and met our friends as planned.

Never, I repeat, never, have I traveled with so much cash on my person. But Japan is a safe country and we had no problems with the yen. Few places were willing to take travelers' checks though.

Learning about the Netherlands

On April 24, 2000, we left for our first Interhostel program. Despite some early differences with the Elderhostel program many years ago, both organizations continue to thrive. Elderhostel is much, much bigger and sponsors many more programs, but both focus on us "oldsters" and have good substantial programs. The one we took to Holland was no exception. It was an excellent program.

We saw much of Western Holland under the general guidance of an enthusiastic adult education specialist, together with some 31 retirees from all around the States. We were based in a big camping motel and bungalow complex, about forty-five minutes from the Amsterdam Airport. Each day we went out on trips emphasizing various aspects of life in the Netherlands.

Our trip was timed for tulip time and we were based in the tulip growing part of the country. Our base was just across the road from tulip fields and we were taken to a small tulip farm and saw the operations first hand. I was surprised to learn that the bulbs we buy are, in most cases, three years old. We saw huge swaths of vibrant colors in the fields. Most of the blooms are cut to allow the plant to put the nourishment back into the bulb. A few small starter bulbs will develop and the best will be planted, along with the previous year's small bulbs. They are dug up and sorted and replanted with only the best ones being sold. There are regulations on pesticide use.

Dutch Tulips

One of the highlights was the visit to Kuekenhof Gardens which is a huge, multi-acre series of beautiful tulip gardens. Our accommodations were sufficiently close to the gardens that we passed their parking lots on several more days and we can testify that a large number of tour busses and people visited the gardens during the two months a year that they are open in the spring.

Almost all the time we were in the Netherlands, we were well below sea-level. They have been controlling the water for years. It is not only the ocean they have to contend with, but several rivers including the Rhine, which brings the melting waters from the European mountains. The rivers have to be channeled for the tides which come upstream twenty or thirty miles. From what I could learn, they apparently do not have much of a problem with water coming up from the water table, but rather they have to deal with too much water from three different sources; the water that falls as rain, the water that comes from the sea, and the water from melting snow in the mountains. This is very different from our problems in Kansas, where we desperately need water to irrigate. They have so much water they have to get rid of some.

We had a field trip to the Delta Project, which is where they have built a tremendously long series of dams to prevent major flooding from the ocean. They have built a sea wall for protection from the storm water. The sea wall gates are lowered only infrequently when the forecasters say it is necessary to prevent flooding. The ocean waters used to cause flooding a number of years ago, but gone are the days when the valiant little boy of yesteryear bravely kept his finger in the dike to keep Holland from flooding. The size and proportions of this engineering feat were impressive. They had to develop a base on the ocean sand floor that could support these multi-storied concrete towers against the surging ocean storm waters. They brought in twenty ton stones from other countries for their base and then developed some "rock mattresses" with small rocks in some strong covers to keep the stones in place. This became the base onto which they brought huge concrete towers which had to be put in the precise proper places to allow the installation of huge multi-ton metal dams that move up and down between these towers that form the sea wall to resist the storms from the North Sea.

We saw a completely different kind of water project in the north of the country. They have built a huge long causeway to close off a portion of the North Sea and have made it a fresh water lake and in some instances have reclaimed the land which can now be farmed. Later cities may even be built on it.

This business of living below sea level has all kinds of complications, but it makes for pretty and useful canals and water all around. We were given the canal tour in Amsterdam and a wonderful tour of the Rotterdam harbor. Rotterdam Harbor is second only to Hong Kong in the amount of shipping that originates there.

An unusual place we visited was the world's largest flower market in the outskirts of Amsterdam. It was reported to be 127 football fields big, and all under cover. We walked around on an elevated walkway with occasional listening stations. We could press a button to select the language for hearing about the activities below. Hundreds of workers on the ground level below us were moving racks of flowers on large dollies. There were at least three large lecture-like halls where we could watch through the glass, the auctions taking place. We were told that 90% of the cut flowers of Western Europe pass through this market. In the auction halls, registered bidders sat with controls that allowed them to enter electronically their bid for whatever quantity they chose. Uniformed attendants brought out the flowers being sold. A new bridge and conveyor belt system was being built to allow the flowers to be moved directly to the nearby Amsterdam airport.

We visited many museums and saw some famous pieces, including some modem art which I confess I could not appreciate. We went to the Pilgrim father churches in Leyden where we saw the plaque commemorating Pastor Robinson, the leader of the American Pilgrims. We later went to their second church in Delft. Our timing in Leyden happened to coincide with the Dutch Queen Juliana's birthday. We stood on the curb waiting to see the Queen's bus go by. It went so fast that we did not really get to see the queen. We stood next to and visited with a youngish woman who said she felt better, even just having seen the Queen's entourage. Incidentally, as a part of our program, we had a lecture on the Dutch Royal family. It seems to be weathering modern times better than the royal family in England.

I must mention that one day we were taken to Het Loo, which is the Palace of the Dutch Royals and not unlike Windsor around London. The Gardens were especially nice and the history of the palace over the years was most interesting. Napoleon had established a relative there as king and they redid everything in the French style. When the Dutch got back in control of things, they redid the gardens to their style, which we were told was exemplified by the three "S's"—Symmetry, Simplicity, and Symbolism - the taste of the Dutch.

I was much surprised to learn that one of our lecturers turned out to have been a student of mine, at KU, some thirty years ago — I confess I did not remember him, but he did remember me.

One of the little discomforts of the program was that the restaurant where we had most of our meals had changed hands since the previous year. It had become an Indian restaurant where we got only spicy Indian food for five or six days until we mounted enough complaints that we got the menu changed more to our liking.

Norwegian Coastal steamer to the tip of Norway

We arranged space on one of the older ships of the Norwegian Coastal Steamer Line. Before bridges were built, enabling more land delivery, this line was the only way to get mail, fish, freight and other goods to the cities and towns all along the coast. We were fascinated to watch what they still delivered at each port along the way on our journey.

We were with our friends, the Andersons. Believe it or not, our friend Andy travels with a fish hook and line. He threw his line overboard and he caught a 12 to 15 pound fish in a very short time. The chef prepared the fish for our dinner!

We were in one of the fjords on the longest day of the year, and were able to see the midnight sun. It didn't get dark at all in those days. We watched the sun barely skim the horizon as it "set" and then begin its rising climb immediately. The captain was asked whether the sun was rising or setting, and he replied, "I can't tell, but does it matter?"

We took this trip to the northern-most point of Europe, in the same year we took the trip to the southern-most point of Africa where we had seen the two oceans meet at Cape Point in South Africa.

Sicily

Most people are familiar with the 1066 Norman Conquest of England, but until this Elderhostel trip we did not know of other Norman conquests. In Sicily we visited two adjoining bishoprics where there had been a rivalry between two Norman Catholic Bishops. Each bishop was intent on building a Cathedral, second only to Saint Peter's in Rome. The results were most spectacular. The cathedral in each bishopric was most gloriously beautiful and grand in the highest. In our travels we had been privileged to see St Peters in the Vatican and marvel at its beauty. The Sicilian "challengers'" cathedrals were beautiful and grand but clearly less dramatic and attractive than St. Peters.

We saw spectacular Greek and Roman temple ruins as well as excavations that were unearthing remnants of many previous civilizations including the Phoenicians and others who had also reigned over this land at some stage.

Western Turkey

Our guide, Leyla, made our three-week-long Elderhostel trip in Western Turkey most memorable. We saw the ruins of some seven civilizations, covering many centuries. Each day, as the bus moved along to our next stop, Leyla came to our seats, answered questions, and told us about our next site.

Me in Turkey

Typically, after a stop somewhere, once all of our group was reassembled on the bus, Leyla asked if everything was all right. On the first day of April, we all came up with several complaints and problems when she asked this. Afterward we explained about April Fool's Day jokes – and she was much assured. Later that day, our bus was back-firing and then it stopped. The bus driver was unable to get it started again, and said it might be a problem with the gas. He had us all get off the bus and push it. We were unable to budge it. We looked up to see the two drivers laughing uproariously. They then admitted that they knew about April Fool's Day and it had all been a joke. We all had a good hearty laugh and the one driver laughed so vigorously that he was literally doubled up – his head almost touched the ground!

Some of the highlights of that trip were visiting the palace and the room where, according to legend, Alexander the Great cut the Great Gordon Knot. We also visited the town where King Midas lived. The river that runs through this town is said to have little specks of alluvial gold dust in its waters. This is also probably the origin of the legends about Jason's Golden Fleece – the sheep probably picked up gold flecks in its fleece from wading in this river. We stood on the Windy Walls of Troy and saw whirling dervishes, a Sufi order of mystics that do whirling dances in praise of Allah, at their headquarters in Central Turkey.

PART 8:

Reflections and Retirement

My Views on Life, Religion and God

I believe that religious belief about God and spirituality, creation, and the after-life is a very private matter and I am very uncertain about it.

I believe firmly there is a God, though I do not view Him as a "person." There is however just too much order--way too much order--in the Universe for it just to have happened.

My dear wife identifies with the views of the Congregational Church. She needs and wants it in our lives, and togetherness has led me to attend our Plymouth Congregational Church. Left alone I would probably join our local Unitarian Fellowship. As a student at the University of Illinois I attended the campus Unitarian church. My Aunt Lillian, an ardent Baptist, when hearing of me attending the Unitarian services, reluctantly admitted that it was probably better for me to go to some church than none at all. She would have been even more concerned if she knew that our campus Unitarian Minister chose many of his texts from literature other than the Bible.

- My suggestions for a useful code of conduct for life in general can be crystallized as follows:
- Understanding that most, if not all major religions, endorse the Golden Rule – Do unto others as you would have them do unto you.
- In even the most happy marriages and other relationships, each partner needs some privacy and space. Each of the partners needs to interact with others both individually and together. We need to be able to talk things out for ourselves, with an uninvolved third party.

- Don't hesitate to ask questions, even though these may show your lack of knowledge.
- Assume that you are dealing with people who will *not* take advantage of you, in the absence of good evidence to the contrary.
- Follow Shakespeare's advice: "Neither a borrower nor a lender be." This includes borrowing by using plastic credit cards.
- Take time to think through your actions and try to perceive how they must look to others.

Reflections and Forecasts

Looking back over my ninety years, I feel that some important and noteworthy developments have been made in our country.

There have been great changes in the role of women in our society. While maintaining their important places as nurses and teachers, they now become CEO's of major corporations too, and it sometimes appears that their role as wives to their husbands is diminished.

The election of a highly qualified man of color to be President recognizes the gains in the move toward equality of civil rights. Our president speaks most eloquently and effectively, as is especially noted when compared with his predecessor. I thoroughly expect that when historians in 2020 and later rate our Presidents, they will put Obama in the upper third and George W. Bush in the lower third. In Bush's campaign he asserted no interest in nation building, and developed his imperial doctrine of preemption to spread freedom around the world.

Historians will find much evidence of a small cabal led by Vice President Chaney, Wolfiwitz and lesser known others that initiated the attack on Iraq and Hussain, following the 9/11 attacks. Bush was quite willing, maybe even desirous of seeing this as a kind of retaliation for the 9/11 attack. Others noted that the 9/11 attack had been staged by a completely different Muslim state. I view this whole military operation in Iraq as the biggest mistake of the decade. The U.S. public is tending to seeing it so. We seem to have forgotten the Powell Doctrine—you don't go in until you know how you are going to get out.

My Retirement Years

In 1989 I retired at the mandatory age of 70. I have now been retired for almost half as many years as I taught. My retirement has given me time to enjoy my gregariousness and have fun with my compatriots.

The University of Kansas Retirees has a very active retiree's organization - the Endacott Society. We have at least sixteen interest sub-groups which range from Singing for Fun to Domestic Public Policy. I have been active in the Domestic Public Policy Group.

The Retirees Society has special evening lectures with pot luck suppers in which the meat is provided and everybody brings salads, vegetables, and most often many, many deserts. The lectures cover a wide variety of subjects.

After mentioning all this food, I must mention the Lawrence Memorial Hospital has a program called Fitness for Life, in which I go and "fight the machines."

My wife and I still divide up our household chores. One of us prepares meals and the other cleans up. Our life in our 1302 square foot one level duplex is delightfully simple and fully adequate. After all we can only be in one room at a time.

I play bridge every Tuesday from 1:30 to 4:00 with three long-standing friends -- Stitt Robinson, Hob Crockett, and Jim Seaver.

I get the *New York Times* delivered to my door five days a week. I get the weekly Washington Post summary by mail and further try to keep up with what is happening in the world.

Danny and I go to many events and lectures, including some of the widely varied offerings of The Dole Center, where speakers come to address interested members of the public. Some of the most memorable talks we attended include those given by Senator Dole and his wife, former President Clinton, and Madeline Albrecht, former Secretary of State.

In the Presbyterian Manor where we live they advertise that you can "live the way you want." I plan to really test them. Recently I found a statement on the world wide web, that if a white male in the U.S. reaches the ages of ninety, the statistical expectation is that he will reach the age of 94. I'm aiming for 96! I am going to try to live here until I have to be carried out feet first.

"Out, out, and out brief candle..."

William Shakespeare
Hamlet
Act 5, scene 5

PART 9
Timeline

1919	James Westbrook Drury is born on February 22 in East St. Louis, Illinois.
1919-1923	I lived with my parents in a bungalow next to the two-story house of my grandparents
1923-1924	I lived about a block south in a two-story up-and-down flat
1924-1927	I lived on 40th Street in the Pearing house
1927-1929	I lived in Vandalia, Mo. My father and uncle had the Ford Motor Agency
1929	My family moved to the "Bluffs," on the hills above East St. Louis where my father operated a small chicken farm
1929-1936	We lived at 1728 North 48th Street in the Village of Washington Park, a suburb of East St. Louis. I attended Hawthorne Grade School, Landsdown Jr. High School and East St. Louis Senior High School
1936-1939	I attended the University of Illinois, in Champaign-Urbana and received a BA and MA
1940-1941	Graduate work at Princeton
1941-1945	Served in the U.S. Army, entering as 2nd Lt and was promoted to Major upon release from active duty. Subsequently I stayed in Reserves and was discharged as Colonel.
1943	Married Florence Mary Daniels in Washington D.C.
1946-1947	Studied and taught at Princeton University
1947-1948	Instructor at the University of Kansas
1947-1951	Lived at 4F Sunnyside in university student housing
1948	Jonathan Daniels Drury was born
1948-1952	Assistant Professor, University of Kansas
1951-1958	Lived in house at 1648 Mississippi. Rented to Ketzels for one year while we were in Japan
1952	Jane Elizabeth Drury was born
1952-1961	Associate professor, University of Kansas
1954-1955	Lived in Japan as visiting Fulbright Professor
1957	Ann Bernice Drury (Heyse) was born

1958-1965	Owned 1613 West 15th Street. We rented out the house while we lived in West Pakistan. We were bought out by Jayhawk Towers
1961-1962	Lived for 531 days in Lahore West Pakistan
1961-1989	Professor, University of Kansas
1965-2002	Lived at 1906 Marvonne.
1965 and 1966	Spent summers in Costa Rica on KU exchange
1971	Jon married Liesel Eiselen (mother of Danelle and Deline) in South Africa on June 26
1980	We lived in Poland for three months, while I taught at the University of Warsaw
1981	Our first grandchild, Danelle was born to Jon and Liesel in South Africa
1982	Ann married David Heyse
1985	Twins, Deline and Dieter were born to Jon and Liesel in South Africa. Dieter died at five months of age
1986	Jon married Claire de Villiers (mother of Alyssa)
1987	Benjamin Chet Heyse was born to Ann and David
1988	Jane married Russ Amos
1989	Jonathan James Heyse was born to Ann and David
1989	Professor Emeritus, University of Kansas
1990	Alyssa Joy Drury was born to Claire and Jon; Lesli Danielle Amos was born to Jane and Russ
1991	Matthew Thomas Heyse was born to Ann and Dave
1993	Sean James Amos was born to Jane and Russ. We celebrated our golden (50th) wedding anniversary;
1996	Claire Drury died of breast cancer, age 42
2002	Jon married Eleonora Viljoen
2003	We moved to the Presbyterian Manor in Duplex E1. We celebrated our 60th wedding anniversary
2004	Jon moved back to Kansas, after retiring from the University of South Africa
2008	Deline Drury married Crae David Nourse on April 5; We celebrated our 65th wedding anniversary.
2009	I celebrated my 90th birthday on February 22.